ISRAEL REBORN

70

YEARS OF MIRACLES

#1 *NEW YORK TIMES* BESTSELLING AUTHOR

MIKE EVANS

TIMEWORTHY
BOOKS

P.O. BOX 30000, PHOENIX, AZ 85046

Israel Reborn: Seventy Years of Miracles
Copyright 2017 by Time Worthy Books
P. O. Box 30000, Phoenix, AZ 85046

Hardcover: 978-1-62961-149-5
Paperback: 978-1-62961-150-1
Canada: 978-1-62961-151-8

This book is dedicated to
the Honorable David Friedman,
U.S. Ambassador to Israel—
a man of integrity who loves Israel,
a man I am pleased to call "friend."

PSALM 102:18−22

This will be written for the generation to come,

That a people yet to be created may praise the LORD.

For He looked down from the height of His sanctuary;

From heaven the LORD viewed the earth,

To hear the groaning of the prisoner,

To release those appointed to death,

To declare the name of the LORD in Zion,

And His praise in Jerusalem,

When the peoples are gathered together,

And the kingdoms, to serve the LORD. (NKJV)

Ms. Retta Zerth
115 Buckingham Dr
Monticello, IN 47960

PREFACE

JUST AS GOD BLESSES those who stand with Israel, so He has blessed His chosen people. Media focus on this tiny Middle Eastern country is normally consumed with conflicts between the Jews and their neighbors who decry the very existence of God's chosen people. Rather than be cowed by all the negative attention derived from international criticism, Israelis have chosen to take the high road and continue to produce inventions and discoveries, and boast a society that benefits the world population in general.

The culture of Israel combines some of the best of Eastern ethnic and religious traditions, along with those of Western civilization. The cities of Tel Aviv and Jerusalem are considered by most to be the artistic centers of the country.

Ethnicity is represented by immigrants from five continents and more than one hundred countries. Significant subcultures are added by the Arabs, Russian Jews, Ethiopian Jews, and the ultra-Orthodox. All the while, it is a family-oriented society with a strong sense of community.

In the nineteenth and twentieth centuries, the then-existing culture was infused with both the mores and traditions of those who had lived outside Palestine, or modern Israel. David Ben-Gurion led the trend of blending the many immigrants who began arriving from Europe, North Africa, and Asia into one melting pot that would unify newer immigrants with veteran Israelis.

At the end of World War II with all its horrors of the Holocaust, devastated Jewish survivors in Europe longed for a return to their homeland. Their dreams were to be delayed when Great Britain was placed in control of Palestine by mandate of the United Nations, and with a growing dilemma: How to walk the tightrope between world opinion and the Arab nations. After the shock and revulsion of the Holocaust, much of the world increasingly demanded that the Jews be allowed to return to their homeland in Palestine—arguably thought to be a place of safety for them. Arabs in the region were adamantly opposed to the move. Greatly frustrated by the situation, the British announced in February 1947 that control of Palestine would be ceded to the United Nations, even then a hotbed of anti-Semitism.

Journalist Eric R. Mandel tellingly wrote of the cultural relativism that still today grips the UN:

> Non-democratic states overwhelmingly control the UN. They often mouth the words of moderation, but defend nations that give sanctuary to terrorists.

How else can one explain that some of the most odious nations on earth are elected to the UN Human Rights Council? In fact, Israel's judge and jury at the UN are often nations that enable terrorism and anti-Semitism.

To accurately judge the United Nations, we need a definition. If Israel is treated and judged completely differently than other nations and held to a standard not applied to any other member nation, then that should be considered anti-Semitism.[1]

In November 1947, the UN offered a plan for partition that would divide the region into an Arab state and a Jewish state, calling for British troops to leave Palestine by August 1948. The Jews welcomed the proposal; the Arabs scorned it. Some British leaders felt it would be impossible for a Jewish state to flourish in the face of such hostility from the Arabs.

In the interim, Jewish leaders moved forward with plans for statehood. A provisional government was established under David Ben-Gurion in March 1948. Two months later, on May 14, as Egyptian fighter-bombers roared overhead and British troops readied for departure, Ben-Gurion and his political partners gathered at the museum in Tel Aviv:

At 16:00 [4:00 PM], Ben-Gurion opened the ceremony by banging his gavel on the table, prompting a spontaneous rendition of Hatikvah, soon to be Israel's national anthem, from the 250 guests.[2]

For two thousand years, Israel had been a nation in exile; overnight it had astonishingly become an autonomous state on the world stage.

But, the following day, Israel was attacked by the five Arab nations that ringed her borders: Egypt, Syria, Transjordan, Lebanon, and Iraq.

When the nation of Israel was reborn on May 14, 1948, it was evidence of God's fidelity to His Word and a clear statement that there is, indeed, hope and redemption available for this world. He said so in His Word and cannot lie:

> God is not a man, so he does not lie.
>
> He is not human, so he does not change his mind.
>
> Has he ever spoken and failed to act?
>
> Has he ever promised and not carried it through?
>
> Numbers 23:19 NLT

The claim to Zion has been reinforced by archaeological discoveries: A Hebrew University archaeologist discovered a Jerusalem city wall from the time of King Solomon (tenth century BC), and said the finding "is the first time that a structure from that time has been found that may correlate with written descriptions of Solomon's building in Jerusalem."[3]

Artifacts found inside excavations around the City of David and within the Old City, the Temple Mount, and Solomon's Stables date the Jewish presence in Jerusalem as far back as 1000 BC, during the time of King David.[4]

As further indications of early Jewish habitation of Zion:

> In April 2005, a series of relics dating back to the periods of the First and Second Temples in Jerusalem were found in piles of rubble which had been discarded at a garbage dump in the Kidron Valley by the Waqf authorities, the Islamic trust responsible for the oversight of the Islamic edifices on the Temple Mount. As excavation has not been possible on the Temple Mount because the Waqf will not permit it, these discoveries are the first of their kind.[5]

The former head of the Israel Antiquities Authority called the removal and dumping of these artifacts "an unprecedented archaeological crime."[6] Archaeologists at the site discovered pottery dating to the Bronze Age and First Temple periods and more than one hundred ancient coins, including some from the Hasmonean Dynasty. One coin from the period of the First Jewish Revolt against the Romans reads, "For the Freedom of Zion," and was created before the destruction of the Second Temple in AD 70.[7]

"For the Freedom of Zion!" Down through the centuries, the Jewish people have cried and prayed for just such freedom. From the building of Solomon's Temple to its destruction in 586 BC to the completion of the Second Temple in 516 BC, from exile to Babylon to the return of the Jews to Jerusalem under Cyrus the Great, Jews have yearned for their homeland and for Zion. This has, without a doubt, been the visible answer to the return of the Jewish people to the land of the patriarchs!

It was toward Zion that the Jews prayed daily. It was of Jerusalem that the psalmist wrote:

> If I forget you, O Jerusalem,
>
> Let my right hand forget its skill!
>
> If I do not remember you,
>
> Let my tongue cling to the roof of my mouth—
>
> If I do not exalt Jerusalem
>
> Above my chief joy.   (Psalm 137:5–6 NKJV)

> On the holy mountain
>
> stands the city founded by the LORD.
>
> He loves the city of Jerusalem
>
> more than any other city in Israel.
>
> O city of God,
>
> what glorious things are said of you!
>
> (Psalm 87:1–3 NLT)

God promised the Land to the children of Israel as their birth-right. Although they have been dispersed throughout the nations as punishment for turning from God, the birthright, the covenant, has never been revoked. The Land does, indeed, belong to the Jewish people.

HEBREW WRITINGS refer to Israel as the "navel" of the world, with Jerusalem at its center. The *Amidah* (Eighteen Benedictions) dating from the Pharisaic Synagogue is the central prayer of Jewish liturgy. It contains prayers for the restoration of the Jews to their homeland. Among its pages is the call to return the exiles, restore David's kingdom, rebuild the temple to its former glory, and remember the observance of Passover, Pentecost, and the Feast of Tabernacles in Zion (Jerusalem).

Abram of the Old Testament, later renamed Abraham by God, was a wealthy man in the village of Haran. Conservationist Walter Clay Lowdermilk wrote:

> The movement for "a Jewish homeland in Palestine" [began four thousand years earlier] when Abraham, prompted by Divine inspiration, left the plains of Mesopotamia to establish a new people on the land of Canaan.[8]

It is actually improper to refer to Abraham, Isaac, or Jacob as "Jewish." The terms "Jew" and "Judaism" were not generally used until hundreds of years later—during the time of the tribe of Judah. Yet all three patriarchs were both the physical and spiritual fathers of Judaism.

Abram, a righteous Gentile, was born in the year 1948 *from* Creation[9] (circa 1800 BC), which points prophetically to the rebirth of the State of Israel in AD 1948. He was the son of Terah, a seller of idols in Ur, one of the largest cities in the region. Former pastor and author Ray Stedman wrote of the city:

> The city of Ur was once thought to be the dwelling place of a primitive people living in mud-walled houses. Accordingly, some scholars once regarded Abraham as a primitive and unlearned man. But the spade of the archaeologist has since turned up ruins of Ur and dispelled this false impression. We now know that Ur was a city of great wealth and culture, home to a library and a university. The people of Ur were devoted to commerce, learning, and the pagan worship of the moon goddess.[10]

Perhaps it had been from early childhood that Abram questioned his father's dedication to gods fashioned of stone and wood. Had he begun to seek the truth and come to believe that his surroundings, the earth and sky, were the work of one Creator? Had he shared this concept with others? However his spiritual upheaval had come about, it may be noted that it was not Abram who sought Jehovah, but God who reached out to *him*.

I envision Abram sitting on a bench outside the front flap of his tent. Sarai, his wife, is likely overseeing the servants as they go about their daily tasks—winnowing grain, hauling water for the animals, spinning cloth, or roasting a goat or camel. Perhaps God had approached others who failed to answer His call, but obviously the Creator saw a trait in Abram that prompted Him to say something like, "That's My man! He's the one with whom I'll make a covenant." Suddenly Abram found himself in an encounter with Jehovah God. He must surely have been stunned to hear the voice of the Lord calling to him:

> Now the LORD had said to Abram: "Get out of your country, from your family and from your father's house, to a land that I will show you. I will make you a great nation; I will bless you and make your name great; and you shall be a blessing. I will bless those who bless you, and I will curse him who curses you; and in you all the families of the earth shall be blessed." (Genesis 12:1–3 NKJV)

God gave Abram three edicts: Go, acquire, multiply. The patriarch-in-training was to leave his country where idol worship was widely accepted; leave his family and its social status; and leave his father's house and the business of making and selling idols. In exchange, Jehovah promised that Abram would become the father of a great nation. What did Abram do? He responded with great faith.

Imagine the conversation he must have had later that day with Sarai: "Wife, we're leaving first thing in the morning. God told me to go. Have the servants take down the tents, gather the flocks, pack everything, and load the camels."

"Abram, what do you mean we're leaving? We can't leave; I'm meeting my friends for lunch tomorrow. What am I supposed to tell them? Where are we going? How long will we be gone?"

"Yes, Sarai, we are leaving, and we won't be coming back. God promised me that He would lead us to the promised land—the land of Canaan. I just know I have to follow His instructions."

"Which God told you that? Where is Canaan, Abram?"

"I don't know, dear. God will direct us as we go; I just know we have to go."

But even after the direct call from God, Abram continued to linger in Ur. It was his father, Terah, who finally stepped in, packed up the family, and headed toward Haran. It was there, halfway to obedience, that Abram and Sarai settled down for a time. Only after his father died did Abram decide to set out for the land God had promised. He was seventy-five years old when he, Sarai, and his nephew Lot packed up "all their possessions that they had gathered, and the people whom they had acquired in Haran, and they departed to go to the land of Canaan" (Genesis 12:5 NKJV). Abram's complete trust in God and his ultimate obedience are unique in Scripture, although he did include Lot and *his* father in the group even after God had instructed him not to bring any relatives (Genesis 12:1). By the time Abram had reached the promised land, he and Lot had acquired so much cattle and livestock that they were forced to separate.

Genesis 13:5–11 paints the picture of the family feud that arose and its resolution:

> Lot also, who went with Abram, had flocks and herds and tents. Now the land was not able to support them, that they might dwell together, for their possessions were so great that they could not dwell together. And there was strife between the herdsmen of Abram's livestock and the herdsmen of Lot's livestock. The Canaanites and the Perizzites then dwelt in the land. So Abram said to Lot, "Please let there be no strife between you and me, and between my herdsmen and your herdsmen; for we are brethren. Is not the whole land before you? Please separate from me. If you take the left, then I will go to the right; or, if you go to the right, then I will go to the left." And Lot lifted his eyes and saw all the plain of Jordan, that it was well watered everywhere (before the LORD

destroyed Sodom and Gomorrah) like the garden of the
LORD, like the land of Egypt as you go toward Zoar. Then
Lot chose for himself all the plain of Jordan, and Lot jour-
neyed east. And they separated from each other. (NKJV)

When Lot stood on a promontory overlooking the land, he must
have noted only the outward appearance of the area—the topography,
the apparent wealth. He could not have seen what Jehovah saw: "Now
the people of Sodom were wicked and were sinning greatly against
the LORD" (Genesis 13:13 NIV). So Lot began his slow descent from the
top of the mountain into the valley below—into a place of carnality,
compromise, and collapse. He would ultimately lose everything he
held dear—wealth and social status, as well as his wife and daughters.
It seemed to be Abram's assignment to rescue his wayward nephew,
first from the captivity by marauding kings, and finally from divine
retribution.

Following Lot's departure and the later destruction of Sodom and
Gomorrah, God again spoke to Abram:

Lift your eyes now and look from the place where you
are—northward, southward, eastward, and westward;
for all the land which you see I give to you and your
descendants forever. And I will make your descendants
as the dust of the earth; so that if a man could number
the dust of the earth, then your descendants also could

ISRAEL REBORN

be numbered. Arise, walk in the land through its length and its width, for I give it to you. (Genesis 13:14–17 NKJV)

After this land grant was bestowed upon him, Abram's name was changed to Abraham, for God had declared that his servant would be "a father of many nations" (Genesis 17:4 NKJV). At the same time, He changed Sarai's name to Sarah (princess), and announced that she and Abraham would have a son. The news must have come as a great shock for both.

Sarah's desperation propelled her to offer Hagar, her Egyptian handmaiden, to Abram as a surrogate. Despite Sarah's interference, there is a lesson to be learned here. In her misery, Sarah turned from faith in God, from dependence on Jehovah, to works—dependence on self. She had a plan and nothing was going to deter her from seeing it come to fruition. Hagar represents works—man or, in this instance, woman—taking matters into their own hands. Abraham could have said, "No." He could have reminded Sarah that God had made a promise to him and he would continue to believe God. That didn't happen. When presented with a pretty little doe-eyed handmaiden, Abraham capitulated.

By the time Hagar was heavy with child, Sarah was consumed with jealousy, and Abraham was forced to endure the contentious atmosphere he had helped create within the camp. It continued to roil within him even after the babe was born.

23

Ishmael was the result of that liaison. A man of faith, Abraham acted instead in his own imprudence rather than following God's direction. He justified a foolish action through moral relativism, tradition, and human reasoning. He was trying to secure God's blessing on his own terms. It was not until some years later when the son of promise, Isaac, was born that Abraham fully realized the gravity of his mistake.

Soon Abraham reached the age of ninety-nine and Sarah eighty-nine, both obviously well past normal childbearing age. Then came the day when Sarah awoke to find that she was pregnant in her old age. She who had laughed at the pronouncement that she would bear a child, she who had intervened and proposed her own plan for an heir, was now carrying Isaac, the son of promise. Not only had God taken away her barrenness, He provided the strength for Sarah to carry the child to term and to bring him forth. God's plan for Abraham and his seed would produce a miracle child.

Soon the trouble with Hagar and Ishmael became increasingly apparent. Eight days after Isaac was born he was circumcised, and after the babe was weaned, Abraham hosted a huge celebration for the son born to Sarah. One day Sarah spied Ishmael mocking Isaac. At that moment, her anger reached volcanic proportions and she exploded. Sarah demanded that Abraham literally drive Hagar and her son from the encampment with only what bread and water they could carry. Abraham had to bear the pain, heartache, and tragedy of losing Ishmael as he complied with Sarah's demands.

God had fulfilled his vow, and soon after the child, Isaac, arrived Abraham set about to teach God's covenant promises to his son. And then horror descended into Abraham's life:

> Then [God] said, "Take now your son, your only son Isaac, whom you love, and go to the land of Moriah, and offer him there as a burnt offering on one of the mountains of which I shall tell you." (Genesis 22:2 NKJV)

We often underestimate just how outrageous this must have seemed to Abraham. It seems impossible to believe that he didn't question God's directive, but the narrative doesn't suggest that. (Neither is there any mention of whether he told Sarah of God's command.) You and I have read the rest of the story and know the outcome—Abraham knew only what God had demanded of him. Yet verse 3 says:

> So Abraham rose early in the morning and saddled his donkey, and took two of his young men with him, and Isaac his son; and he split the wood for the burnt offering, and arose and went to the place of which God had told him. (Genesis 22:3 NKJV)

Rejecting the "son of human reasoning," God made a covenant with Isaac, the "son of faith." Ishmael became the father of the Arab race, and Isaac a patriarch of the Hebrews. The Quran teaches that Ishmael, not Isaac, was the son of promise, and that he inherited the land and the title deed to Jerusalem. The battle continues even today.

This time Abraham did not argue nor did he hesitate to obey God's directions. He didn't bargain with God; he didn't ask for anything in return for his obedience. Instead, he immediately made arrangements for the three-day journey to Mount Moriah. I believe Abraham's heart had to have been so heavy it was difficult for him to place one foot in front of the other. I believe he was puzzled about God's plan. Abraham was not some superman—a spiritual hero with mystical powers—he was "everyman" and he was about to offer the child of promise. How would you feel if you knew you were about to lose a beloved son or daughter? Abraham was surely no different.

So, off they set on a three-day hike across the desert terrain—a journey of some sixty miles—to the place designated by God. When they arrived, Abraham asked the servants to wait while "the lad and I will go yonder and worship." Then he added what might well be a hint to the strength of his faith, "and we will come back to you." (Genesis 22:5 NKJV)

After three days of spiritual wrestling with God, Abraham was assured that God would provide. As he unloaded the wood from the donkey and laid it on Isaac's back, the lad asked, "Look, the fire and the wood, but where is the lamb for a burnt offering?"[11] And in verse 8 with great conviction and complete assurance, his father replied,

"My son, God will provide for Himself the lamb for a burnt offering." Abraham had not figured out just how God would provide—a lamb wandering by, Isaac raised from the dead, a last-minute stay of execution—but he was convinced that God would provide!

I have a mental picture of father and son slowly trudging their way up the mountain to the place where God finally says, "Here; this is it." When they arrived, the father and son set about gathering stones to erect an altar to Jehovah. Abraham carefully laid the wood and knelt before his son. He gently bound Isaac's hands and feet and laid him on the altar. Now, Isaac was old enough to run for his life. Not only did Abraham display unparalleled obedience, so did his beloved son, Isaac.

Just as Abraham raises the knife to plunge it into Isaac's heart, an angel of the Lord cries, "STOP! Don't hurt the boy."

> And He said, "Do not lay your hand on the lad, or do anything to him; for now I know that you fear God, since you have not withheld your son, your only son, from Me." (Genesis 22:12 NKJV)

Abraham must have heard something rustling in a bush near the altar. He looked around and there, held fast, was a ram caught by its horns. With unparalleled gratitude, Abraham untied his son, bound the ram, and laid it on the altar as a sacrifice to his faithful Jehovah-Jireh—his provider.

2

JEHOVAH ALREADY had a plan in place to spare Isaac, the son of promise in order to fulfill His covenant with Abraham. While much has been said in modern times about the Jews fleeing to Palestine for safety from persecution, pogroms, and the Holocaust, Abram was certainly not a refugee running for his life when sent forth in search of God's promised land. He had no need: He was wealthy and well respected in Ur. He went in faith only because God directed him to go.

It is important to note that the land given to Abraham and his descendants was a relatively small area when compared to that occupied today by Arab tribes. It is also notable that neither loss of their homes nor exile because of rebellion and disobedience had any effect on God's promise of ownership of the land. The Bible does not indicate that the Jewish people had any desire to increase the area God had defined for them to occupy.

The *Torah*—the first five books of the Old Testament and Moses' record of the travels of Abraham's descendants—shows their steady march toward the promised land. When Moses led the exodus of the children of Israel out of bondage in Egypt, the group had grown from less than one hundred to more than 600,000 men, plus an untallied number of women and children. Standing atop Mount Nebo in western Jordan, Moses reiterated the boundaries God had set for the promised land.

The *Torah* is impregnated in the genes of the Jewish people—those who practice their religion as well as those who do not. The longing to return to Zion, the land from which they were exiled and to which they have always belonged, is as innate as the need for food and water. It is their biblical, cultural, and political heritage. In Deuteronomy, chapter 34, Moses wrote the finale of God's grand production of leading His children from Egypt to Canaan:

> Then Moses went up from the plains of Moab to Mount Nebo, to the top of Pisgah, which is across from Jericho. And the LORD showed him all the land of Gilead as far as Dan, all Naphtali and the land of Ephraim and Manasseh, all the land of Judah as far as the Western Sea, the South, and the plain of the Valley of Jericho, the city of palm trees, as far as Zoar. Then the LORD said to him, "This is the land of which I swore to give Abraham, Isaac, and Jacob, saying, 'I will give it to your descendants.'"[12]

Jacob's son Joseph was sold by his brothers into slavery and was, according to God's plan, taken to Egypt. While there, he was reconciled to his family and moved all—seventy in number—to the land of Goshen to protect and preserve them from a famine that gripped the land. In Genesis 15:12–14 NKJV, God said to Abram:

> Know certainly that your descendants will be strangers in a land that is not theirs, and will serve them, and they will afflict them four hundred years. And also the nation whom they serve I will judge; afterward they shall come out with great possessions.

This passage goes on to say:

> On the same day the LORD made a covenant with Abram, saying: "To your descendants I have given this land, from the river of Egypt to the great river, the River Euphrates." (Genesis 15:18 NKJV)

Jacob's offspring were warned that they would be removed from the land if they disobeyed God's commands. The Bible also foretells that a Jewish remnant would be restored to the promised land after a worldwide exile, as has miraculously occurred in our day:

> For I will take you from among the nations, gather you out of all countries, and bring you into your own land.

. . . 'Thus says the Lord God: "On the day that I cleanse
you from all your iniquities, I will also enable you to dwell
in the cities, and the ruins shall be rebuilt. The desolate
land shall be tilled instead of lying desolate in the sight
of all who pass by. So they will say, 'This land that was
desolate has become like the garden of Eden; and the
wasted, desolate, and ruined cities are now fortified and
inhabited.'" (Ezekiel 36:24, 33–35 NKJV)

Since the 1900s Jews have returned to the promised land from
nations around the globe. When the nation of Israel was reborn on
May 14, 1948, it was evidence of God's fidelity to His Word and a clear
statement that there is, indeed, hope and redemption available for
this world.

Columnist Charles Krauthammer wrote graphically of the land
today:

Israel is the very embodiment of Jewish continuity:
It is the only nation on earth that inhabits the same land,
bears the same name, speaks the same language, and
worships the same God that it did 3,000 years ago. You
dig the soil and you find pottery from Davidic times, coins
from Bar Kokhba, and 2,000-year-old scrolls written in
a script remarkably like the one that today advertises ice
cream at the corner candy store.[13]

The Jews, under Roman rule, lived very orderly and relatively stable lives. However, those placed in authority over Jerusalem were often greedy and bereft of knowledge of Mosaic law. Because of their lack of understanding, the Romans were prone to confer insult rather than honor. Civil war raged from time to time, launched by Zealots attempting to overthrow Roman rule. The uprisings were often suppressed with massacres that left legions dead.

The last king to rule Judah was Herod Agrippa, the son—or grandson—of Herod. (Herod had been well known for his incestuous habits, so it is within reason to believe that Agrippa could have been a son.) Although appointed by the Romans to rule the region, Agrippa was identified as a righteous king and frequently received favorable comments. Under his kingship, it appears that the relationship between the government in Rome and the religionists in Judea had turned a corner and were, at least, harmonious if not overtly friendly.

According to the Jewish Virtual Library:

> The three years of Agrippa's reign were a period of relief and benefit for the Jewish people of Judea. The residents of Jerusalem were exempted from the impost on houses. . . . He omitted the patronymic [surname] "Herod" from coins minted for him and followed a markedly pro-Jewish policy when he was required to arbitrate disputes between Jews and non-Jews . . . Agrippa made frequent

changes in the appointment of the high priest. He was highly sympathetic to the Pharisees and was careful to observe Jewish precepts. He married his daughters to Jewish notables, and withdrew his consent to the wedding of one daughter to Antiochus, king of Commagene, when the latter refused to be circumcised.[14]

Sent to Rome as a child, Agrippa became acquainted with a nephew of Augustus Caesar, Gaius Julius Caesar Augustus Germanicus, or, as he was known, Caligula ("little boots," a moniker he despised). The connection between Agrippa and Caligula would later avert a brawl in Judea after the death of Emperor Tiberius. Caligula was known by numerous epithets: unhinged, unstable, insane, mad. He declared himself to be a living god. He had his nephews, who stood between him and the throne of Tiberius, murdered, paving the way to the lofty position of emperor with the blood of his relatives. Caligula was the personification of insanity and his bloody reign one of utter horror. According to author Michael Farquhar, "Caligula had the heads removed from various statues of gods and replaced with his own in some temples."[15]

During his rush to be seen as a living god, Caligula dictated that his statue be placed in the temple in Jerusalem, where the Jews would be required to worship the man. Such a move was guaranteed to spark rebellion in the region: "Accordingly he sent Petronius with an army to Jerusalem to place his statues in the temple, and commanded him that, in case the Jews would not admit of them, he should slay those that opposed it, and carry all the rest into captivity."[16]

Into that quagmire stepped Agrippa. Figuratively laying his own head on the block, he petitioned Caligula not to move forward with desecrating the Jewish temple. The emperor acquiesced and the order was rescinded, making Jerusalem the only city in the Roman Empire without a statue of Caligula. After approximately four years on the throne in Rome, the emperor's own Praetorian Guard grew tired of his antics and assassinated him.

The Romans were equally brutal toward anyone attempting to foment rebellion in the Jewish ranks. Later, after the dispatch of Agrippa, graft and corruption rekindled the fires of Jewish revolt, and finally the Pharisees joined forces with the Zealots. War broke out in the summer of AD 66. Caught off guard, Roman forces in Judea quickly lost control of the Masada and Antonia fortresses and were slaughtered by the rebels. At Masada, rebels discovered a vast quantity of arms and dried food supplies. Herod the Great had stockpiled the materiel more than one hundred years earlier in preparation for a possible war with Cleopatra. The storehouse proved fortuitous, and Jerusalem was soon back in Jewish hands.

In Jerusalem the leaders of the rebellion coined money, collected taxes, and organized defenses for the entire country. From Rome, Nero dispatched consul Vespasian with several legions to crush the uprising,

M I K E   E V A N S

the most stubborn and desperate revolt Rome had ever faced. Bloody
fighting for the next three years resulted in isolation of the rebels in
Jerusalem and Masada.

In AD 70 Vespasian was crowned emperor and returned to Rome,
leaving his son Titus in charge of the Judean campaign. Titus laid siege
to Jerusalem with eight thousand veteran troops. Fewer than a third
as many Jews defended the city. In the face of incredible shortages
and starvation, they clung tenaciously to their city. By late July, Titus
had captured the Antonia Fortress. The defenders who were hollow-
eyed with hunger regrouped. From the roof of the portico around
the edge of the temple platform they hurled down stones, arrows,
and fiery brands against the legionnaires. The Romans then burned
the roofs from under the Jewish defenders. The attackers gained
access to the platform itself, and the defenders retreated behind the
wall of the temple proper into the Court of the Women and the Court
of Israel. More flaming projectiles set the sanctuary ablaze, and a
bloody slaughter ensued. Biblical scholar Ray Stedman wrote of that
desperate time:

> During the long siege a terrible famine raged in
> the city and the bodies of the inhabitants were liter-
> ally stacked like cordwood in the streets. Mothers ate
> their children to preserve their own strength. The toll
> of Jewish suffering was horrible but they would not

surrender the city. Again and again they attempted to trick the Romans through guile and perfidy. When at last the walls were breached Titus tried to preserve the Temple by giving orders to his soldiers not to destroy or burn it. But the anger of the soldiers against the Jews was so intense that, maddened by the resistance they encountered, they disobeyed the order of their general and set fire to the Temple. There were great quantities of gold and silver there which had been placed in the Temple for safekeeping. This melted and ran down between the rocks and into the cracks of the stones. When the soldiers captured the Temple area, in their greed to obtain this gold and silver they took long bars and pried apart the massive stones. Thus, quite literally, [and as had been foretold by Jesus] not one stone was left standing upon another. The Temple itself was totally destroyed, though the wall supporting the area upon which the Temple was built was left partially intact and a portion of it remains to this day, called the Western Wall [or by some, the Wailing Wall].[17]

Jewish historian Josephus, who had defected to the Romans earlier in the rebellion, was an eyewitness to the event. He claimed that the streams of blood pouring from the corpses of the defenders were more copious than the fire that engulfed everything flammable in the vicinity. Before the Roman legions had finished, the city lay in ruins with the exception of Herod's palace, where the Tenth Legion was stationed as a permanent force of occupation. It would be three more years before the imperial armies recaptured Masada, the last stand of the Jewish revolt. Nearly one thousand men, women, and children had been hiding in this isolated mountaintop fortress. When the Roman soldiers finally scaled the awesome heights and reached the fortress, they were met with an eerie silence. Tragically, all the Jews at Masada had committed suicide, preferring to die at their own hands than be slaughtered by the armies of Rome.

The destruction of the temple began the second exile. The Diaspora scattered the Jews around the globe for the next eighteen centuries, but there was always a remnant in Jerusalem. Others, although separated from their beloved land, never forgot the Holy City or the destruction of the temple. It might have been then that the cry first went forth, "Next year, Jerusalem."

Simon Bar-Kokhba, a charismatic Jewish leader, united the Jews and enticed recruits from throughout the Diaspora, including Samaritans and Gentiles. His troops totaled nearly four hundred thousand when rebellion exploded in AD 132. It took three years and five legions of battle-hardened Roman troops to retake Jerusalem. Bar-Kokhba remained elusive but was eventually captured and executed in AD 136.

Following its victory, the Roman army exacted a terrible revenge. Some of the rebel leaders were skinned alive prior to their executions. Massacres during the fighting had been common; now the survivors were either sold into slavery or simply allowed to starve. Burial was not permitted, so heaps of corpses lay decomposing in the streets and fields. The Temple Mount was literally plowed under and an entirely new city was constructed north of the old one. It contained two buildings, together with pagan temples. The main temple platform served as a public square on the south side of the city. It was bedecked with statues of Hadrian and other Roman notables. An offense punishable by death was established to prevent Jews from entering Jerusalem; neither were they allowed to observe the Sabbath, read or teach the law, circumcise, or otherwise follow God's laws.

Hadrian changed the name of Judea to Syria Palaestina and proclaimed its capital to be Caesarea. Jerusalem would no longer be the capital city. Syria Palaestina is the origin of the name *Palestine* and in modern times applies to the area eventually became the national homeland of the returning Diaspora Jews. It was said that Hadrian renamed Judea after the ancient enemy of the Jews—the Philistines. Romans in general, and Hadrian in particular, despised Jews.

Of all the nations conquered by the Romans, the Jewish people remained the only group that would never fully submit to Roman rule. For that reason, Hadrian was determined to erase the memory of Judea and its people from the pages of history. For the next five hundred years, Jews would only be allowed in the city of Jerusalem on the anniversary of the burning of the temple.

The Jews would be deprived of their homeland and self-rule until May 14, 1948, when the dream of returning became a reality. What many today seem to overlook is that Israel didn't just rise from the rocky land of Palestine in 1948; it has been in existence for millennia, although known by various names and always with a remnant of Jews in residence in the land.

Israel is not merely a long, narrow strip of land on the Mediterranean Sea; she represents only a part of the divine land grant—from God to the descendants of Abraham, Isaac, and Jacob:

On that day the LORD made a covenant with Abram and said, "To your descendants I give this land, from the Wadi of Egypt to the great river, the Euphrates—the land of the Kenites, Kenizzites, Kadmonites, Hittites, Perizzites, Rephaites, Amorites, Canaanites, Girgashites and Jebusites." (Genesis 15:18–21 NIV)

It was a gift from Jehovah, and the ownership of Israel's land is and has always been nonnegotiable.

At Camp David in July 2002, President Bill Clinton almost succeeded in dividing Jerusalem. He placed a pen in the hand of PLO Chairman Yasser Arafat, urging him to sign the agreement that would have accomplished that. Arafat refused to sign. The president was shocked. If Arafat had complied, Jerusalem would have been divided. All Christian sites would now be under

Islamic rule of law! This includes Mount Calvary and the Garden Tomb, and even the Christians who live there. America was challenging God Almighty and His prophetic plan. Never a wise thing to do.

Why did Arafat not sign the agreement? He wanted not only ALL of the temple site, but ALL of Israel's land! Those who take a stand against Israel fight God Almighty. The son of Abraham and Hagar will not win in a battle against Jehovah. Why? For thousands of years, the offspring of Ishmael have spoken curses over Jacob's seed. When the wars of the Middle East have finally ended, Jacob's sons will rule. Who will win the conflict in the Middle East? Those who bless Israel will be triumphant. Who will lose the battle in the Middle East? Ultimately, those who fight the children of Israel will go down in defeat. God created Israel; God defends Israel.

In March 2002, Oklahoma Republican senator James Inhofe addressed the issue of Israel's right to her land:

> Every time there is a dig in Israel, it does nothing but support the fact that Israelis have had a presence there for 3,000 years. The coins, the cities, the pottery, the culture—there are other people, groups that are there, but there is no mistaking the fact that Israelis have been present in that land for 3,000 years. It predates any claims that other peoples in the region may have.

The ancient Philistines are extinct. Many other ancient peoples are extinct. They do not have the unbroken line to this date that the Israelis have. Even the Egyptians of today are not racial Egyptians of 2,000, 3,000 years ago. They are primarily an Arab people. The land is called Egypt, but they are not the same racial and ethnic stock as the old Egyptians of the ancient world.

The Israelis are in fact descended from the original Israelites.[18]

When you sign your name to a check, you represent that you possess the amount indicated on that check. God wrote His name in Jerusalem, and He has the power and authority over that which His name represents.

3

ON MAY 13, 1948, the day before the British Mandate was to expire, David Ben-Gurion, the executive head of the World Jewish Organization and chair of the Jewish Agency for Palestine, declared the establishment of a Jewish state in *Eretz Yisrael*. It was to be known as the State of Israel.

But just who was this David Ben-Gurion, and how did he become germane to Israeli politics? He was born in 1886 in Plonsk, Poland, then part of the Russian Empire, to Avigdor and Scheindel Grün (Green). His mother would die when David was eleven.

The child learned Hebrew in Russia at the age of three. When he was a teen, his father wrote to Theodor Herzl asking his advice on the gifted youngster's education. Little did his father know that in less than fifty years, his son would be an instrument used by God to birth the modern nation of Israel. In 1903, David was convinced of his belief in a Jewish state, but in 1904 at the age of eighteen he found himself in the streets of Warsaw, hungry and struggling to earn enough to buy food. Even with minimal education, he worked as a teacher and strove to further his education despite limitations on Jews attending Russian schools. As he became more and more aware of growing anti-Semitism in his world, he and two friends established a youth club, *Ezra*, to promote Hebrew studies and encourage Jews to immigrate to the Holy Land, which only whetted his own appetite to leave Poland behind for Palestine. While studying at the University of Warsaw, David joined *Poalei Zion*, the Social-Democratic Jewish Workers' Party.

When news reached him that his champion, Theodor Herzl, had died, David was overcome with grief. He explained his sadness to a friend:

> Only once in a thousand years is a man of miracles such as this born. Like the expanse of the sea is . . . our loss. [He called Herzl] the great fighter and hero who . . . awoke a people dwelling in tombs from the slumber of death.[19]

Eighteen months later, David would set out upon his journey to Palestine, eventually assume the mantle of Herzl, and help bring about the birth of his hero's dream—a homeland for the Jewish people.

Soon after his arrival in Palestine, David adopted the surname by which the world would come to know him: Ben-Gurion—translated as "son of a lion cub." He chose that moniker because of a first-century Jewish leader, Joseph Ben-Gurion. David Joseph Ben-Gurion's namesake, King David, had been a successful military leader; he hoped to achieve that same notoriety.

Writer and biographer Shabtai Teveth wrote of the impact Ben-Gurion's early years would have on the future prime minister:

> For Ben-Gurion, the first things were also the final ones, and what filled his early years occupied his world forever. The foundation for his life's work was his formidable personality . . . [described as] currents of tenderness and love, confidence in his singularity, and the glimmerings of a dream of the rebirth of Israel all combined in a mixture miraculously suited to his mission.[20]

By 1919 Ben-Gurion began working for the underground, fighting for his dream. He settled into a tiny apartment in Jerusalem and indulged himself by buying books. He catalogued his collection of books as consisting of more than 777–340 in English, 219 in German, 140 in Hebrew, 29 in French, 13 in Arabic, 7 in Russian, 7 in Latin, 2 in Greek, 1 in Turkish, and 19 in other miscellaneous languages. He spoke each of those languages and was striving to learn Spanish. David realized the gates to Palestine were closed to the Jews of the world, including the United States; but he believed with all his heart that Israel would be reborn.

In 1929 Arab violence broke out in Jerusalem and quickly spread to other cities in Palestine. The grand mufti of Jerusalem spread rumors that Jews intended to occupy the Al-Aqsa Mosque on the temple site. All told, more than 130 Jews had been killed throughout the country within seven days before British troops finally brought the situation under control. Ben-Gurion mobilized an army of farmers to defend the Jewish people—not only against the Arabs but the British as well. He traveled throughout Europe in March 1933 declaring, "We urgently need living Jews to return to Palestine."

In 1934 Ben-Gurion declared in a speech:

> The tragedy that has struck the Jews of Germany has not struck alone. Hitler's regime endangers Jews everywhere... Hitler's regime cannot exist for very long before embarking on a war of revenge against France, Poland and Czechoslovakia, and other neighbouring countries where Germans live or against vast Soviet Russia. Germany will not go to war today because she is not prepared. However, she is preparing... it does appear that the danger of war today is as great as it was in 1914.[21]

When David arrived in the Palestine then under the control of the Ottoman Empire, he joined forces with agricultural workers to establish communes, which ultimately became the kibbutzim. To his thinking, there was only one way to truly follow Zionism: take control of the Land by employing Jewish labor. David also became involved in pro-independence and socialist activities. By the start of World War I, he must have been on any list of people most likely to be a disruptive influence. He and Yitzhak Ben-Zvi (instrumental in forming the Jewish defense group *Hashomer* and Israel's second president after its rebirth) were soon apprehended and deported by the Ottoman rulers.

Jewish refugees streamed into Palestine from Germany and Central Europe, threatened by Nazi Germany's territorial ambitions. The numbers increased from 200,000 in 1930 to 400,000 by 1936.

Unwelcome and ousted from Palestine, Ben-Gurion traveled to New York City to plead the Zionist cause to Jews in the United States. While there, he met and married Paula Monbesz, who was also involved with the *Poalei Zion* organization. David and Ben-Zvi returned to Palestine in 1918 as members of the Jewish Legion in the British Royal Fusiliers, brainchild of Russian Zionist Ze'ev (Vladimir) Jabotinsky. The two men had left Ottoman-controlled Palestine only to return to a land under the jurisdiction of the British.

Back in the Holy Land and still believing it would be Jewish labor that would provide the bedrock foundation for a new state, Ben-Gurion dove right into local politics. He established trade unions, specifically the General Federation of Labour, or *Histadrut*. As its representative, David attended World Zionist Organization and Jewish Agency meetings. In 1935, he was elected chair of both groups.

47

Ben-Gurion's stance in reference to Arabs in Palestine was strengthened following the 1936 Arab Revolt. Mufti Haj Amin al-Husseini, who headed the Arab High Command, called for a work outage and a boycott against all products made by Jews. This quickly spiraled into attacks targeting both the British and the Jews. As the influence of Haj Amin and frustration with European oversight grew, the number of extremists burgeoned exponentially.

In July of 1937, the Peel Commission (Palestine Royal Commission)—"a British Royal Commission of Inquiry, headed by Lord Peel, appointed in 1936 to investigate the causes of unrest in [British Mandate for Palestine] following the six-month-long Arab general strike in Mandatory Palestine"[22]—issued a report detailing the British despair of ever finding a solution to the Arab-Jewish conflict. Britain had made irreconcilable commitments to both groups. Since the British were unwilling to subject four hundred thousand Jews to Arab domination, or conversely to place nearly a million Arabs under Jewish rule, the only apparent solution was partition—to divide the territory into two separate states. Jerusalem and Bethlehem, said the Royal Commission, should be set aside in a British enclave with access to the coast.

The League of Nations rejected the partition concept. King Abdullah of Transjordan and his friends, the Nashashibis, likely favored the move but were afraid to say so. The mufti and his followers were contemptuous in their rejection, which assured that the

Arab Higher Committee would also turn it down. The Jews were willing to accept it as the least undesirable alternative. It was all a moot point; the status quo would continue. That would mean more fighting.

Also in July, Haj Amin stopped in to see the German consul general in Jerusalem. He wanted to tell the Nazi official how much he admired the Third Reich, and how he would appreciate a little help in his struggle against the British and the Jews. From there the negotiations progressed until Admiral Wilhelm Canaris, head of German intelligence, delivered quantities of weapons from German manufacturers to the mufti via Iraq and Saudi Arabia. Finally, in the wake of the assassination of several British officials in Galilee by Arab gunmen, the British deposed the mufti and abolished the Supreme Muslim Council and the Arab Higher Committee. The mufti retreated to the sanctuary of the Dome of the Rock.

On October 15, 1937, Haj Amin slipped past British police disguised as a beggar. He got to Jaffa by automobile and then was smuggled aboard a fishing boat to Lebanon. Haj Amin kept retreating north until, by 1941, he emerged as the honored guest of Adolph Hitler in Berlin. Amin was convinced that the Nazis held the key to the two great goals of his life—to destroy the Jews and to drive the British out of the Middle East.

When the League of Nations was established in 1937, the British were convinced that Palestine must be divided between Arabs and

Jews. Ben-Gurion, too, believed that was the only solution and wrote to his son, Amos:

> Erect a Jewish State at once, even if it is not in the whole land. The rest will come in the course of time. It must come."[23]

The British, faced with the rise of Germany and Adolph Hitler by 1939, proposed an Arab state with the Jews as a minor populace. Ben-Gurion was convinced that no one would come to the aid of the Jewish people.

Dan Kurzman, a foreign correspondent, wrote of Ben-Gurion:

> The full impact of his lifelong obsession with the Bible struck with blistering force when it appeared that Jerusalem would fall to the Arabs and perhaps be lost forever to the Jewish state. Whatever happened to any other Jewish areas, the Holy City must be saved. It was the soul of the Jewish people, the fount of the light to be cast unto the nations. He had agreed that it be internationalized as a temporary concession. But an Arab flag over Jerusalem? Not for one minute![24]

Following that period, Ben-Gurion's ideology was transformed to the belief that war was the only solution and that the end would come only when either the Jews or Arabs won. He crusaded unstintingly for Zionist ideas and ideals both in the United States and in Europe, as he also worked tirelessly to develop military strength in Palestine. At the onset of the Second World War, he actively encouraged Palestinian Jews to enlist in the Allied cause. At the same time, he was busy organizing an underground railroad to liberate Jews from the Nazis and help them escape to Palestine. Following the end of the war, as resistance against British rule became the focus, Ben-Gurion strongly denounced right-wing extremists who resorted to terrorism to make their case.

4

ADOLF HITLER was the man whose name will forever be linked to the start of World War II in 1933 until his death by suicide in 1945. He was responsible for the deaths of eleven million people—among the dead, six million Jews—during the Holocaust. Hitler was born in Braunau am Inn, Austria, on April 20, 1889, and was the son of Alois Schicklgruber Hitler and Klara Pölzl, both from a remote area of lower Austria. Hitler's father had been born out of wedlock to a young peasant woman, Maria Anna Schicklgruber. It was not until Alois was in his thirties that his father returned to the village, married Maria Anna, and changed the young man's last name to Hitler. Had he not come forward to claim an inheritance, Johann Hitler's grandson would have grown up as Adolf Schicklgruber. One can't help but wonder if he would have had the same impact and garnered the same notoriety had he retained that name rather than the more familiar moniker by which he became known.

As a child, Adolf was said to have been angry and sullen, undependable, short-tempered, and indolent. He was antagonistic toward his father, who was a strict disciplinarian, and intensely devoted to his industrious mother. The young Hitler "took singing lessons, sang in the church choir, and even entertained thoughts of becoming a priest."[25] He was devastated when his mother died during his teen years.

When he was sixteen, Adolf made his way to Vienna with dreams of becoming an artist. He applied to the Viennese Academy of Fine Arts, but was roundly rejected by that august body. He survived in the large, cosmopolitan city by doing odd jobs and selling sketches in backstreet pubs. Between sketching patrons, he would spout political rants of his ostentatious dreams for a superior Germany to anyone too drunk to walk away.

Adolf was enchanted with the manipulative methods of Vienna's mayor, Karl Lueger, and quickly adopted his affinity for anti-Semitism, with its fanatical demand for "purity of blood." From the eccentric teaching of an excommunicated monk, Lanz von Liebenfels, to those of German Nationalist Georg von Schönerer, the impressionable young Hitler adopted the radical belief that the Jewish people were responsible for anarchy, dishonesty, and the ruination of civilization, government, and finance. According to those so-called "learned men," the only purpose of the Jew was to completely weaken Germany and dilute the superior Aryan race.

Hitler joined the Sixteenth Bavarian Infantry Regiment during World War I, where he served as a dispatch runner. He was awarded the Iron Cross for bravery but was caught in a gas attack shortly before the end of the war. He spent months recovering from the effects, which included temporary blindness. After his recovery and still in the military, he was delegated the job of spying on various political factions in Munich—among them the German Workers' Party.

Hitler joined the other forty members of that small group in 1919 and the name was changed shortly thereafter to the National Socialist German Workers' Party. By 1921, he had claimed the chairmanship of the organization and began to dazzle crowds with his formidable gift of oratory. Soon thereafter, the party had adopted a new logo—the swastika, which inexplicably resembled an Indian religious symbol—and which Hitler believed would symbolize the triumph of the Aryan man. It also adopted a new greeting, *"Heil!"* and eventually *"Heil, Hitler!"* (This can be translated as "Hail Hitler," or more ambiguously as "Salvation through Hitler.")

The mustachioed little man mesmerized his listeners with his gravelly, impassioned voice—never mind that his rants contained little of actual value. Near the end of 1921, he had come to be known as *der Führer,* or "the leader." He formed gangs to maintain control at his assemblies and to apply goon-squad tactics to disrupt those of his adversaries. These were the beginnings of the infamous storm troopers, the SS, Hitler's black-shirted and dreaded bodyguards.

In 1922 Hitler had almost presciently outlined his plan fully in a conversation with a friend, appropriately named Joseph Hell:

> If I am ever really in power, the destruction of the Jews will be my first and most important job. As soon as I have power, I shall have gallows after gallows erected, for example, in Munich on the Marienplatz—as many of them as traffic allows. Then the Jews will be hanged one after another, and they will stay hanging until they stink. They will stay hanging as long as hygienically possible. As soon as they are untied, then the next group will follow and that will continue until the last Jew in Munich is exterminated. Exactly the same procedure will be followed in other cities until Germany is cleansed of the last Jew![26]

Hitler infamously declared the Jewish people to be Germany's Public Enemy No. 1, the race accountable for all the nation's internal problems. He strongly stressed what he saw as "the anti-Semitism of reason" that must lead "to the systematic combating and elimination of Jewish privileges; its ultimate goal the total removal of the Jews."[27] He was so convinced Germany was near collapse, that he joined forces with nationalist leader General Erich Friedrich Wilhelm Ludendorff in an attempted coup.

The ensuing riot that began in a Munich beer hall resulted in (1) the deaths of sixteen individuals, (2) the Nazi Party being outlawed, and (3) Hitler being tried and sentenced to five years in prison. The riot would forever afterward be known as the "Beer Hall Putsch," a violent attempt to overthrow the government. Inexplicably, his sentence was commuted to nine months.

During his incarceration, Hitler dictated a draft of *Mein Kampf* to Rudolf Hess, a devoted sycophant. The tome—filled with a coarse, ill-conceived jumble of anti-Semitism, fabrication, and fantasy— evolved into the literal bible of the emerging Nazi Party. By 1939, this hodgepodge of pretense had sold five million volumes and had been translated into eleven languages. Even today that infamous tract is widely read and even taught in schools of some Middle Eastern countries.

British-born German philosopher Houston Stewart Chamberlain wrote to encourage Hitler in a letter dated October 7, 1923. He zeal-ously advised the Führer that he was perceived as the "opposite of a politician . . . for the essence of all politics is membership of a party, whereas with you all parties disappear, consumed by the heat of your love for the fatherland."[28] In a later missive to Hitler, Chamberlain asserted: "One cannot simultaneously embrace Jesus and those who crucified him. This is the splendid thing about Hitler—his courage. In this respect he reminds one of [Martin] Luther."[29] It is quite obvious from his writings that Chamberlain agreed with Hitler's assessment of the Jews' place in German society.

The German heirarchy made what would soon become a disastrous error in judgment in 1925. They removed the prohibition against the Nazi Party and granted permission for Hitler to address the public. Coincidentally, when he needed it most in order to expand the reach of the party, a worldwide economic crisis reached Germany. Ironically, the resulting magnitude of unemployment, panic, and anger afforded Hitler the timely opportunity to step forward and claim his perceived role of redeemer and savior of the nation. On January 30, 1933, Weimar Republic of Germany's president Paul von Hindenburg was persuaded to nominate the Führer as Reich Chancellor. The result: Germany had lost its last chance to avoid a Second World War—and the Holocaust.

Hitler's determination to outfox his opponents and remove the conservatives from any role in the government took little time or effort. He abolished free-trade unions, removed Communists, Social Democrats, and Jews from any participation in politics, and brutally consigned his rivals to concentration camps. He further solidified his hold on Germany in March 1933 with the use of persuasive argument, indoctrination, fear, and coercion. The façade was firmly in place, and the people of Germany were intimidated into subjugation.

With the death of von Hindenburg in June 1934, the Third Reich was commanded by a determined dictator who held the reins both of

Führer and chancellor, as well as all the powers of the state accorded to a leader. Hitler abandoned the Treaty of Versailles, conscripted a massive army, supplied it with war materiel, and in 1938 forced the British and French into signing the Munich Agreement. Soon to follow were laws against Jews, more concentration camps, the destruction of the state of Czechoslovakia, the invasion of Poland, and a nonaggression pact with the USSR. The only obstacles standing between Hitler and the rest of the world were the trio of Franklin D. Roosevelt, Winston Churchill, and Joseph Stalin, along with the armies of Western civilization.

Just one week after Roosevelt was sworn in for his first term as America's chief executive, German laborers had completed Dachau, the original concentration camp. Within its confines some 40,000 individuals, most of them Jews, would be murdered. Hitler would follow the opening of that camp by nationalizing the Gestapo and bringing it under his full control. Just three months later, he had successfully combined all commands under the aegis of the Nazi Party.

In 1935, the Nuremberg Laws were instituted and German Jews lost their citizenship with its rights and privileges. They were now totally under the iron fist of Hitler and his rabid Jew-hatred. Like many of the Jews in the earlier days of Hitler's rule, Roosevelt was initially deceived by the picture presented to the world at the 1936 Olympics. American historian and author Deborah Lipstadt wrote:

The sports competition was a massive exercise in propaganda and public relations, and many American reporters were uncritical about all that they saw. . . . Americans, particularly non-German speaking ones who only knew Germany from the Games—departed convinced that the revolutionary upheavals, random beatings, and the murders of political opponents had been greatly exaggerated or were a thing of the past. Those bedazzled included not only the athletes and tourists, but personages such as newspaper publisher Norman Chandler and numerous American businessmen. This period marked the beginning of Charles Lindbergh's love affair with the Reich. One reporter was convinced that as a result of the Games visitors would be . . . inclined to dismiss all anti-German thought and action abroad as insipid and unjust. [The visitor] sees no Jewish heads being chopped off, or even roundly cudgeled. . . . The people smile, are polite, and sing with gusto at the beer gardens. Visitors to Berlin described it as a warm, hospitable place and Germany as a country well on its way to solving the economic and unemployment problems which still plagued America.[30]

Even the events of *Kristallnacht* in 1938, in which the Reich looked the other way while a rabid mob of its citizenry attacked Jews and their businesses throughout the country, did little to move other world leaders toward a more proactive stance on rescuing European Jews caught in Hitler's reprehensible assault. Franklin Roosevelt had entered the office of the presidency with no firm policy regarding the Jews and a Palestinian homeland. It was not until the early months of 1939 that Roosevelt expressed any interest in the manifest destiny of the Jewish people.

5

HITLER'S PLAN to destroy the Jews was a public relations triumph for the German Führer. He employed rhetoric that compared them to a cancer destroying Germany from within, and complained constantly of the need to eliminate the deadly "disease" from the country. His tactic to paint the Jewish population as responsible for every ill that the German people faced provided the rationale for the near destruction of an entire race of people in Europe.

After years of this continuous rhetoric, it took only ninety short minutes for Hitler's henchmen to determine the fate of six million Jews. During that period, roughly the time it would take to drive from Jerusalem to Tel Aviv during peak traffic time, the Holocaust became a heinous reality.

The date: January 20, 1942.

The place: The beautiful Wannsee Villa located in a serene lakeside suburb of Berlin.

The objective: To find a "Final Solution to the Jewish Question."

Presiding over the conference was SS Lieutenant General Reinhard Heydrich, chief of the Security Police and Security Service. In attendance were fourteen high-ranking German military and government leaders, among them Adolf Eichmann. Imagine: Over lunch, fifteen men in ninety minutes changed the world in ways that even *they* could not have imagined. January 20, 2017, marked the 75th anniversary of that fateful conference. We dare not let this dubious anniversary pass without marking how little time it takes to alter the course of history.

Perhaps Raul Hilberg, Holocaust expert, wrote most convincingly of the trials and tribulation that awaited the Jews from the time of Constantine's conversion:

> Since the fourth century after Christ there have been three anti-Jewish policies: [forced] conversion, expulsion, annihilation. The second appeared as an alternative to the first, and the third emerged as an alternative to the second. . . . The missionaries of Christianity had said in effect: You have no right to live among us as Jews. The secular rulers who followed proclaimed: You have no right to live among us. The Nazis at last decreed: You have no right to live. [31]

As events of the 1930s led ominously toward a Second World War, the Nazis under Hitler had already been searching for a "final solution" for what they considered the Jewish problem. As the meeting began in 1942, Heydrich was determined that none should doubt his superiority or his authority, which was not limited by geographical borders. He briefed those in the room on the measures that had already been taken against the Jews in an attempt to eradicate them from both the German culture and homeland.

Initially, steps had been implemented to allow German Jews to immigrate to whatever countries would accept them, but the move proved to be too slow for the Führer and the Reich. Now the men gathered to implement Hitler's new solution. Heydrich provided a list of the number of Jews in each country; a total of eleven million Jews were to be involved. In his zeal he determined:

> In large, single-sex labor columns, Jews fit to work will work their way eastwards constructing roads. Doubtless the large majority will be eliminated by natural causes. Any final remnant that survives will doubtless consist of the most resistant elements. They will have to be dealt with appropriately, because otherwise, by natural selection, they would form the germ cell of a new Jewish revival.[32]

Translation: All will die.

According to the recovered minutes of that meeting, Jews were to be purged, beginning in Germany, Bohemia, and Moravia. After that, they were to be expunged in Europe from east to west. Many questions arose as to how to identify those who were to be considered Jews. That issue was not resolved during the Wannsee meeting.

Of course, this was not the beginning of the extermination of the Jewish people. Many of those in attendance had already participated in the murders since the summer of 1941. Even before the gathering at Wannsee, more than a half million Jews had been murdered behind army lines. The question was how to attain the goal of mass extermination in areas outside the battle zone. A more efficient way needed to be found to eliminate larger numbers. No, the meeting was not called to determine how to begin the process but rather to spell out how the "final solution" would be achieved. By January, death camps equipped with gas chambers were under construction.

The ordinary citizenry of Germany certainly did not enter the war determined to annihilate six million of their neighbors. It began with a subversive program of anti-Semitism aimed at blaming the Jewish people for all the ills that had beset Germany following its losses in World War I. Perhaps even Hitler did not initiate the plan with total extermination in mind. That seed began to germinate only after Jews were denied entry into other countries. It seemed to him that he had been given a green light to do whatever he wished with Germany's Jewish population.

There are so many questions that arise regarding Hitler's assumption of power in Germany, but perhaps one of the most chilling is: Where was the church at that time? Author Victoria J. Barnett wrote of the role of the church during those dark and devastating years:

> European Jews [were] not a high priority of the Allied governments as they sought to defeat Hitler militarily. The courageous acts of individual rescuers and resistance members proved to be the exception, not the norm. . . . this inertia defined the organized Christian community as well. Churches throughout Europe were mostly silent while Jews were persecuted, deported and murdered. In Nazi Germany in September 1935, there were a few Christians in the Protestant Confessing Church who demanded that their Church take a public stand in defense of the Jews. Their efforts, however, were overruled by Church leaders who wanted to avoid any conflict with the Nazi regime. Internationally, some Church leaders in Europe and North America did condemn the Nazis' measures against the Jews, and there were many debates about how Christians outside Nazi Germany and Nazi-occupied territory should best respond to Hitler's brutal policies. These discussions, however, tended to become focused

more on secondary strategic considerations—like maintaining good relations with colleagues in the German Churches—than on the central humanitarian issues that were really at stake. . . .

Reflecting on the failure of the Churches to challenge the Nazis should prompt us to ponder all the others—individuals, governments and institutions—that passively acquiesced to the Third Reich's tyranny. Even the wisest and most perceptive of them, it seems, failed to develop adequate moral and political responses to Nazi genocide, failed to recognize that something new was demanded of them by the barbarism of Hitler's regime. [33]

Hitler was aided in his quest for world domination by a Western media determined to bury its head in the sand. One of the most prominent was the *New York Times*, which seemed unwavering in underplaying the horrors taking place in a Nazi-controlled Germany. According to Northeastern University journalism professor Laurel Leff:

The story of the Holocaust made the *Times* front page only 26 times out of 24,000 front-page stories. . . . In only six of those stories were the Jews identified on page one as the primary victims. Nor did the story lead the paper, appearing in the right-hand column reserved for the day's most important news—not even when the concentration camps were liberated at the end of the war. . . . the *New York Times* was less likely than other news organizations to miss what was happening to the Jews. But it was also more likely to dismiss its significance. . . . the newspaper's Jewish publisher believed the Jews were neither a racial nor ethic group, and therefore should not be identified as Jews for any other than religious reasons. . . . The result: *The New York Times* was in touch with European Jews' suffering, which accounts for its 1,000-plus stories on the Final Solution's steady progress. Yet, it deliberately de-emphasized the Holocaust news, reporting it in isolated, inside stories. The few hundred words about the Nazi genocide the *Times* published every couple [of] days were hard to find amidst a million other words in the newspaper. *Times* readers could legitimately have claimed not to have known, or at least not to have understood, what was happening to the Jews.[34]

6

KING SOLOMON wrote in Proverbs 29:18, "Where there is no vision, the people perish" (KJV).

The prophet Isaiah foresaw the rebirth of the nation of Israel. *The Message* records the event this way:

> Before she went into labor, she had the baby. Before the birth pangs hit, she delivered a son. Has anyone ever heard of such a thing? Has anyone seen anything like this? A country born in a day? A nation born in a flash? But Zion was barely in labor when she had her babies! (Isaiah 66:7–8)

On May 14, 1948, after almost 2,900 years, the Jewish people reclaimed their homeland. During a day's time—twenty-four hours—the nation of Israel was miraculously reborn. The United Nations had issued a mandate, the British had withdrawn, Gentile control of the land had ceased, and Isaiah's prophecy had come to fruition.

God gave the prophet Habakkuk a vision of redemption:

> For the vision is yet for an appointed time; but at the end it will speak, and it will not lie. Though it tarries, wait for it; because it will surely come, it will not tarry. (Habakkuk 2:3 NKJV)

In the 1800s, long before the events of 1948, a cause was born. It set the stage; it attracted the men and women who would be instrumental in the rebirth of Israel. They had caught the vision of God's plan to restore His chosen people to their homeland. In October 1943, in the midst of World War II, three men—British prime minister Winston Churchill, Deputy Prime Minister Clement Atlee, and World Zionist Organization's president, Chaim Weizmann—sat down in London to discuss the latest partitioning plan, which called for Jerusalem to be a separate territory under a British high commissioner. The plan would have to be kept secret until after the war, Churchill explained, but he wanted the other two men to know that Israel had a friend in him. He explained that when Hitler had been crushed, the Jews would have to be reestablished in the land where they belonged. Churchill added:

I have an inheritance left to me by [Lord Arthur] Balfour [writer of the Balfour Declaration], and I am not going to change. But there are dark forces working against us. [35]

Dated November 2, 1917, the declaration was a letter from Lord Balfour to Lord Walter Rothschild detailing British backing for the rebirth of a homeland for the Jews in the Middle East. It persuaded the League of Nations to entrust the United Kingdom with the Palestine Mandate in 1922.

Prime Minister Churchill probably didn't know how dark and powerful those forces were. No matter how firm his commitment to Zionism, the British Foreign Office and the authorities in Jerusalem who had charge of the Mandate hindered him from stating his position. The all-too-familiar story of the bitter struggle and disappointment for the Jewish people continued—Palestine would not be opened to the hapless survivors of the concentration camps.

In the months between November 29, 1947, when the UN General Assembly voted for partition, and May 14, 1948, when the last British troops left and the State of Israel was reborn, Jerusalem was the scene of ongoing conflict.

The tiny, new nation of Israel was dependent on Haganah and its three fighting units for defense: Field Corps, Guard Corps, and the *Palmach*—an elite fighting force. Under Ben-Gurion's leadership,

Palmach would ultimately become the core of the Israel Defense Forces (IDF). Haganah's ranks boasted 60,000 willing fighters, but less than 20,000 were equipped and prepared for the battle that was to come. Yigael Yadin, Haganah chief of operations, informed Ben-Gurion: "The best we can tell you is that we have a 50/50 chance."[36] On May 31, 1948, one of the new prime minister's first directives was to establish the IDF.

The Israel Ministry of Foreign Affairs offers a concise summation of events following the declaration of independence:

> Less than 24 hours later, the regular armies of Egypt, Trans-Jordan, Syria, Lebanon and Iraq invaded the country, [including volunteers from as far afield as Sudan, Pakistan and Yemen] forcing Israel to defend the sovereignty it had regained in its ancestral homeland. In what became known as Israel's War of Independence, the newly formed, poorly equipped Israel Defense Forces (IDF) repulsed the invaders in fierce intermittent fighting, which lasted some 15 months and claimed over 6,000 Israeli lives (nearly one percent of the country's Jewish population at the time).[37]

May 14, 1948, in the US capital dawned unusually warm and humid. The anticipation in government halls was palpable: Would the president recognize a Jewish state or would he acquiesce to his secretary of state and postpone any acknowledgment? Unlike today's "instant news instantly" mind-set, transmission of information in that day took a bit longer. What was going on in Jerusalem? How high was the anticipation there? How great was the threat of annihilation?

Machal (overseas volunteers) poured into Israel from 29 countries, both Jews and Gentiles alike. About 1,200 came from the United States, and 250 from Canada. Another 800 volunteers came from South Africa, 700 from Great Britain, 250 from North Africa, 250 from Latin America, about 500 from France and the rest of Europe. There were some from Australia, the Belgian Congo, Finland, Holland, Switzerland, Italy, and Ireland. There was even a volunteer from the Navajo Indians who served in the Fourth Troop. His name was Jesse Slater. He went into battle with a Navajo charm bracelet, a cross and *mezuzah* worn around his neck. He would say, "You just can't be too careful with all those bombs and bullets flying around." Thirty-one of those who died were pilots. In the beginning, Israel's entire air force was manned exclusively by Machal volunteers.

In Washington, D.C., White House Counsel Clark Clifford was still attempting to sway Secretary of State George Marshall and Undersecretary of State Robert Lovett to the side of recognition. He approached Lovett with the question that if the secretary of state refused to support Truman on the matter, would he at least not openly defy him? After much vacillation, the general finally agreed to do nothing, neither positive nor negative. He would simply make no comment.

Clifford also contacted Eliahu Epstein, head of the Jewish Agency, and requested his assistance:

> Mr. Epstein, we would like you to send an official letter to President Truman before 12 o'clock today formally requesting the United States to recognize the new Jewish state. I would also request that you send a copy of the letter directly to Secretary Marshall. [38]

Working with several advisers, Epstein had drafted a succinct missive that reached the White House by noon on the fourteenth. His request as an agent of the Provisional Government of Israel read as follows:

> I have the honor to notify you that the State of Israel has been proclaimed as an independent republic within frontiers approved by the General Assembly of the United Nations in its Resolution of November 29, 1947, and that a provisional government has been charged to assume the rights and duties of government for preserving law and order within the boundaries. . . . The Act of Independence will become effective at one minute after six o'clock on the evening of 14 May 1948, Washington time. . . . I have been authorized by the provisional government of the new state to tender this message and to express the hope

that your government will recognize and will welcome
Israel into the community of nations.[39]

In the original document, Epstein had referred to the new state
simply as "Jewish state." As the letter was being delivered to Clifford
by aide Harry Zinder, Epstein was advised by shortwave radio that
the official name of the newly established state would be "Israel." He
immediately dispatched a second aide to overtake Zinder, strike over
the phrase *Jewish state*, and insert *Israel* into the document.

At 6:11 that evening, White House Press Secretary Charlie Ross
read the following statement dated May 14, 1948, approved and signed
by President Harry Truman:

> This government has been informed that a Jewish
> state has been proclaimed in Palestine, and recognition
> has been requested by the [provisional] government
> thereof. The United States recognized the provisional
> government as the de facto authority of the new [State
> of Israel].[40]

Just as Epstein's document had the added word *Israel*, so did Truman's document. The United States of America, in the year of its 172nd
anniversary, was the first foreign nation to recognize the sovereign
State of Israel; the USSR followed three days later. The president's
pro-Zionist advisers bore the brunt of criticism for Truman's actions;

however, it was the feisty, fedora-wearing Missourian who made the final decision. Although Truman was the first foreign head of state to acknowledge the new nation, other heads of foreign governments soon took up the gauntlet to ensure that the new nation of Israel would survive.

7

AS PALESTINE MOVED toward partition, one Jewish leader emerged from the pack and stepped onto the stage of political history: Golda Meir. Although born in Kiev in 1898, her family moved to Milwaukee, Wisconsin, when she was eight. At seventeen, Golda discovered her Zionist faith—the doctrine to which she devoted the remainder of her life.

In 1921 Golda and her husband, Morris Meyerson, immigrated to British Mandate Palestine. By 1924, she was immersed in the political scene and by 1928 had become an official in the Histadrut Trade Union. In the early 1930s, she returned to the United States as the trade union's emissary.

After many of the Jewish leaders in Palestine were imprisoned, in 1946 Meir was appointed to lead the Jewish Agency's Political Department as the chief liaison with the British. She actively raised funds to support Israel's War of Independence. During the first *kibbutz* convention in 1922, David Ben-Gurion became aware of Golda's gift of silver-tongued oratory, and appointed her a member of his government.

In the early days of May 1948, Ben-Gurion had asked Golda to masquerade as an Arab, and then dispatched her to a meeting with Jordan's King Abdullah. On May 11, three days before the end of the Mandate, and disguised as a peasant woman, Golda slipped across the Jordan River at Naharayim for a second meeting with the king. Golda and Abdullah had met the previous November. Ironically, the two reunited on a short stretch of land on the east bank of the Jordan River. It was the site of a hydroelectric power station built and run by the Jews, and from which the king's palace received electricity. David Ben-Gurion had sent Golda to meet with Abdullah in the home of the plant's director. They greeted one another much like old friends with a common enemy—the mufti Haj Amin. Abdullah confided that in the event of partition, he would prefer simply to annex the Arab sector to his kingdom.

Abdullah was pale and seemed to be under great strain. Golda asked if he had broken his promise to her—the one made during their visit the previous year. He told her that when he had made that promise he believed he was in control of his own destiny. He had since learned otherwise. He informed Mrs. Meir that he felt war could be averted if the Jews were not in such a rush to proclaim statehood.

Golda replied that the Jews had waited two thousand years to reclaim the land that was rightfully theirs, and she didn't think they were being impatient at all. The time of statehood had arrived; it would not be postponed. The king sadly informed her that war was inevitable. Golda assured him that the Jews would fight...and that they would win. She thought that sounded much better than a separate state led by Haj Amin.

Meir pledged that the Jews would leave the Arab sector to its own devices, and the Jews would devote themselves entirely to the establishment of their own sovereignty within the borders assigned them by the UN. Abdullah was not anti-Semitic; he recognized the Zionists as fellow Semites who had returned to their homeland after a long exile. Their presence in Palestine had already profited him and his people immensely. He knew better than to think he could put a stop to the establishment of a Jewish state. The mufti, on the other hand, was a foolish man who viewed Jews in terms of the pale rabbinical students so easily cowed by his ruffians' clubs. Abdullah knew the Zionists for what they were: a vigorous and capable people who could put up a stiff fight.

When Israel issued its declaration of statehood, Ben-Gurion assumed the joint offices of prime minister and defense minister. He demanded that the various armed factions be merged into one fighting force—the Israel Defense Forces (IDF). He masterminded the creation of many of the burgeoning state's institutions and various internal projects to aid development (i.e., Operation Magic Carpet to airlift Jews from unfriendly Arab countries, the founding of new towns and cities, and a national waterworks along with other infrastructure projects). He continued to encourage pioneering and farming in the remote areas of the land.

Ben-Gurion achieved Theodor Herzl's dream, his passion for a Jewish state, and was then entrusted with its guardianship. The newly acknowledged State of Israel was all that Herzl had imagined. As Yoram Hazony, author, philosopher, and political theorist, wrote:

> Ben-Gurion found himself overseer of a state that was neither neutral nor multinational as Judah Magnes, Martin Buber, Lessing Rosenwald or the ever-present U.S. State Department had hoped to see formed. It was, instead, in the most precise way conceivable the state about which Herzl had written in *The Jewish State*—a place where non-Jewish residents were welcomed "to participate in the up-building of the state on the basis of full and equal citizenship," but one whose significance, single-mindedness, and function would nevertheless result in "the right of the Jewish people to be masters of their own fate . . . in their own sovereign state." [41]

When Ben-Gurion stepped to the podium at 4:00 p.m. on that warm Friday afternoon in May, he carefully read the statement that would declare Israel's sovereignty. The following day, May 15, Egypt launched her military aircraft toward Tel Aviv in retaliation. It was *Shabbat*, and there would be no official response until Saturday at the conclusion of the holy day. As the prime minister again delivered a news bulletin to his awaiting audience, he announced that an Egyptian warplane had been shot down, its pilot imprisoned, and the aircraft added to the Israeli Air Force. He also reported that the United States had been the first nation to recognize Israel's independence.

Ben-Gurion's announcement was the initial step in a war that would last one year, three months, and ten days; it would test Israel's very resolve and preparedness. Azzam Pasha, the Arab League secretary-general incorrectly asserted:

> It will be a war of annihilation. It will be a momentous massacre in history that will be talked about like the massacres of the Mongols or the Crusades. [42]

In an appearance before the UN Security Council, the United States proposed to charge the Arab countries with "breach of the peace." Andrei Gromyko, Soviet delegate to the UN, stated the obvious:

> This is not the first time that the Arab states, which organized the invasion of Palestine, have ignored a

decision of the Security Council or of the General Assembly. The USSR delegation deems it essential that the council should state its opinion more clearly and more firmly with regard to this attitude of the Arab states toward decisions of the Security Council.

At the outset of the confrontation, it was obvious that Israeli forces were greatly outnumbered. One army, alone—the Egyptians—boasted 40,000 ground troops armed with approximately 135 armored fighting vehicles, heavy artillery, and sixty planes in its arsenal—including bombers and single-seat fighter planes. Forces in Egypt and Jordan had been trained and led by British army officers. The Israelis were faced with those daunting figures, yet marched forward determined and unbowed.

Conversely, the Israeli Air Force was nonexistent prior to the attack. That state of affairs was soon rectified by the donation and commandeering of private aircraft quickly assembled from a multinational hodgepodge collection of civilian aircraft. The planes were commandeered or donated and then adapted for use by Israeli forces.

In 1948 Czechoslovakia agreed to sell arms to Israel—at a cost of $40,000 per fighter plane, $10,000 per pilot-training program for two weeks. Yugoslavia also agreed to let the Haganah use its ports and airfields to transship desperately needed military supplies. On May 20, 1948, an Israeli airlift code-named *Balak* using volunteers from the

West began from an airfield in Czechoslovakia to fly critically needed military supplies employing a couple of old Constellations flying the Panamanian flag. By June 11, those two Constellations had made thirty flights and delivered one hundred tons of precious cargo.

When the first Supermarine Spitfire Mk.IX fighters and Avia S-199s (often called "Messerschmitts") landed in Israel from Czechoslovakia, it signaled a real breakthrough for the Israelis. It was the beginning of what is today a well-armed and diverse array of aircraft.

8

COMPARED TO the Arab League, Israel's fighting force was woefully lacking in training, materiel, and funds to wage an ongoing war. Every man was aware of one harsh truth, however: Victory meant survival; defeat meant obliteration. There was only one choice to make: Stand and fight. Combatants from every faction struggled to claim victory on the battlefield, while others were charged with raising funds and obtaining arms.

Over twenty-five hundred years ago, the prophet Isaiah gave a graphic forewarning of events that would take place in Israel's future:

> You shall seek those who contend with you, but you shall not find them; those who war against you shall be as nothing at all. For I, the LORD your God, hold your right hand; it is I who say to you, "Fear not, I am the one who helps you." (Isaiah 41:12–13 ESV)

We see that promise fulfilled repeatedly during the months that Israel faced her foes. On May 19, 1948, Egyptian forces initiated an advance against Kibbutz Yad Mordechai in an attempt to take Tel Aviv. The attack against the 130 residents had been planned to take no more than three short hours; it lasted for days. The tiny band of fighters armed with little more than weapons cobbled together from household items held off the attacking forces much longer than anyone anticipated. The Egyptians were ultimately successful, but the battle delayed the infantry, armored, and artillery battalions. Egyptian morale suffered because of the fierce fighting they had faced from the Jews at Yad Mordechai.

As the war for independence continued to rage, there were numerous other instances that defied the rules of engagement. The Israeli military seemed to have an edge that the Arab League did not, sometimes bordering on the miraculous. It could be said that a series of little miracles conferred the ultimate victory.

An area at the crest of Mount Canaan near Safed provided an almost impenetrable spot from which the Arabs could fend off any ingress into the city. As long as that position was held, opposing forces had the upper hand. That is, until the Israelis brought in a homemade mortar round labeled the *Davidka* (Little David). At worst, it was of little strategic value because its trajectory was inaccurate; at best, it was of psychological value because the mortar was exceedingly noisy.

On one particular Friday afternoon just before Shabbat, the Israelis moved the Davidka near Safed and fired mortars several times. Suddenly, it began to rain—quite the phenomena for days in May or June in Israel. The Arab troops stationed atop Mount Canaan were terrified that the Jews had dropped an atomic bomb. After all, what else would cause rain to fall that time of year? The Arabs hurriedly packed up and moved not only from the mountaintop, but they entirely quit the northern regions of the Galilee.

Moshe Dayan, who would become a household name during the Six-Day War in 1967, was commander in the area around Dagania, the earliest kibbutz to be established in Israel in 1909. Word reached the settlement that Syrian forces were arrayed for an attack. The column of armored troops included forty-five tanks that, if not halted, would cause a devastating blow to the morale of the Israelis.

Dayan called for the use of one of only four howitzers available to all the Israeli troops. Two were dismantled, transported to Degania, and reassembled just minutes before Syrian troops broke through the perimeter established around the kibbutz. Locked and loaded on the advancing Arab army, the Jewish fighters scored a direct hit on the lead tank. Not knowing that the residents of Degania had possession of only the two weapons, the Syrians quickly turned their armored vehicles around and headed back toward their own border.

Perhaps one of the greatest miracles was the liberation of Jerusalem from an Arab boycott. In the early years of the war to retain their independence, Jewish authorities in Tel Aviv had to put Jerusalem on hold while they gave their attention and manpower to ward off an Egyptian onslaught coming up through the Negev. This gave the forces of Abdullah ibn Hussein, *sharif* (governor) of Mecca an advantage in Jerusalem. Because of the Dome of the Rock, it had become the third holiest shrine in Islam. Also, Abdullah's father had lost Mecca and Medina to the Saudis in 1925, so Jerusalem would serve as compensation for his family as well—a vindication of the Hashemite dynasty.

The Arab Legion, Abdullah's army, led by British lieutenant-general John Bagot Glubb, was the only professional army in the Arab Middle East at that time. Glubb was reluctant to commit his Bedouin soldiers to street fighting in Jerusalem. Had he known how poorly defended the city was at that point, he might have felt differently. The first units of the Legion—a small detachment—arrived in the Old City on May 19. At the same time 2,080 of Glubb's soldiers invaded the heights north of the city and began to advance on the New City—the center of Jewish population with roughly 100,000 inhabitants. The Legion's approach struck terror: This was a *real army,* not an undisciplined bunch of irregulars.

Haganah's district commander, David Shaltiel, had roughly the same number of men under his command, but they were virtually weaponless. Glubb's first column of the Legion was met by a group of teenagers armed only with Molotov cocktails, a bazooka, and an armored car. The Jordanians had unwittingly made a wrong turn near the Mandelbaum Gate and were taken completely by surprise by the ambush. Before the Arabs could withdraw, the teenagers had managed to knock out three of their armored cars. The victory gave new heart to the Israelis; they would need it.

While the New City was momentarily made safe from capture by the Arabs, the Jewish Quarter remained in grave danger. On May 18, a second company of Haganah men had managed to fight its way into the Quarter to join the lone company defending the Jews there. Here, however, Glubb's Legion held the real advantage. Its artillery prevented further reinforcement by the Jews, and the Arab death grip inexorably tightened. The Quarter was forced to surrender on May 28. It was an enormous symbolic capitulation not only for the inhabitants of Israel but to the worldwide Jewish community.

Ten days of savage fighting followed, during which the Jews managed to turn back the Arab assault. On May 28, Glubb called off his attack. His men had been seriously mauled in the fighting. Besides, the strategy for his assault had been proven wrong; the battle for Jerusalem would be decided on the heights of Latrun, which overlooked the supply road from Tel Aviv. David Shaltiel believed he had done what he could in the Jewish Quarter and that his primary responsibility was the New City.

The Egyptian threat from the south had been lessened by the end of May, and the Israeli high command could then focus its attention on getting relief to Jerusalem. By early June the Jewish sector had been the recipient of more than ten thousand rounds fired from Jordanian artillery. Two thousand homes had been destroyed with twelve hundred civilian casualties reported. The city was entirely cut off from supplies, and its people were on the verge of starvation.

Haganah operations chief Yadin and Ben-Gurion summoned General Yigal Allon, who had been leading the fighting in Galilee, to head the assault on Latrun and break the Arab stranglehold on Jerusalem's supply route. Haganah troops had been augmented with large numbers of raw recruits, many fresh off immigrant ships. These men were rushed to the front by bus and taxi. In the blistering heat, these untrained troops were tossed into a direct frontal assault on the entrenched Jordanians, lacking badly needed artillery support or even adequate reconnaissance. The Arabs raked them with artillery and mortars. The Jews suffered heavy losses and were forced to withdraw.

In the midst of the campaign to take Latrun, Ben-Gurion assigned a new and special volunteer to oversee the assaults. He was David Daniel "Mickey" Marcus, a Jewish American, West Point graduate, veteran of the Normandy invasion, and a colonel in the United States Army. Marcus had left his prestigious post at the Pentagon to help his brothers in Israel. He joined with Shlomo Shamir, the commander of the first assault against Latrun, and together they plotted to make the next one equally successful.

In spite of reinforcing their operations considerably, the Fourth Regiment of the Arab Legion stood firm in the face of the next Israeli attack; and more Jewish bodies littered the slopes in front of their positions. It seemed that the hope of relieving Jerusalem was being bled dry at Latrun. An upcoming deadline made their task even more urgent: A UN cease-fire was due to go into effect on June 11. When that happened, if the road to Jerusalem was not open, it would be too late.

Marcus began to search for a different route. There was a path by which troops had been getting to Jerusalem on foot. Marcus recruited two young officers, Vivian Herzog and Amos Chorev, to take a jeep ride with him, and together they discovered it was indeed possible to traverse this path from Tel Aviv to Jerusalem on wheels. Now, all they needed to do was make it passable for trucks. Dirty and unshaven from their trek across mountainous terrain, the three men headed directly for Ben-Gurion's office as soon as they arrived back in Tel Aviv. The prime minister listened carefully to the report, probably thinking: *Maybe, just maybe, if a jeep could get through . . .*

A searing heat wave bore down on Palestine that June day as hundreds of workers set out from Tel Aviv to begin the daunting task of building a road in the wilderness. Given the shortage of heavy machinery, it was a mind-boggling job. Meanwhile, in Jerusalem the situation was growing more desperate by the hour; only a few days' supply of food and water remained. The ordnance officer estimated there was enough ammunition for a sustained battle of no more than twenty-four hours.

Dov Joseph, a Canadian Jew and the civilian governor of Jerusalem during the crisis, could take much of the credit for the orderly and disciplined way of life in the city. The people were remarkably steadfast and courageous. On Saturday, June 5, just six days before the UN cease-fire would be imposed, Joseph was still reeling from the fate of his daughter, who had died fighting in the south just a few days prior. Now he was forced to cut the citizens' rations once more. He and his fellow Jerusalemites would subsist on but four thin slices of bread each day, supplemented by half a pound of dried beans, peas, and groats for the week. He waited in anticipation of news from what many were calling the new "Burma Road," the proposed Tel Aviv-to-Jerusalem route. It was named after the path hacked out of jungle-covered mountains in Burma by Chinese coolies in order to provide supplies to Chiang Kai-shek's troops during World War II.

Marcus began the excavation with just one bulldozer at his disposal. The work inched forward at an agonizingly slow pace. Each hundred yards of progress toward Jerusalem required as much as three hundred yards of winding roadway. Alternate crews worked day and night. A second bulldozer became available, but by then conditions in Jerusalem were desperate. On Sunday, June 6, Joseph had cabled Ben-Gurion that the city couldn't hold out beyond the following Friday.

Ben-Gurion weighed his alternatives: Marcus had three miles to go. Could he make it in four days?

Ben-Gurion decided he could not afford to risk the wait. He called out the Home Guard and sent the members on foot, each carrying forty-five-pound packs loaded with food for Jerusalem. Three hundred middle-aged men were bused to the end of the makeshift road and set out to hike the three tortuous miles over ridges and through ravines until they reached the point where they could finally off-load their packs onto a truck bound for the Holy City.

On June 9, Mickey Marcus and his two bulldozers miraculously emerged from the wilderness through which they had been constantly digging since the end of May. The first trucks, laden with food and water, made their way over that primitive roadway to be greeted in Jerusalem with tears and cheers of joy. Two days later, at ten a.m., the UN cease-fire went into effect. Miraculously, it was just the breathing space the Israelis needed to rearm and replenish for completion of the War of Independence.

In Jerusalem, the war was over. The Jordanians held half the city—including the Old City with its holy sites, the Western Wall, the then-abandoned Jewish quarter, and all the surrounding countryside north, south, and east. The Israelis held the New City and a secure western corridor leading to the coast. Sadly, Jerusalem now had a knife thrust through her heart: for the first time in her history, she was a divided city.

9

IN THE SUMMER OF 1948, Count Folke Bernadotte, vice-chairman of the Swedish Red Cross, was chosen by the UN to represent that organization in Palestine. His official title was "United Nations Mediator in Palestine," and his specific task was to negotiate a truce between the Palestinians and the Jews. His plan was to demand that the Jews cede Jerusalem and the Negev to Jordan; they were to receive the western Galilee in return. These were comparable to the initial partition boundaries that had been roundly rejected by all in the region. Once the Arab League had lined up in battle formation against Israel, perhaps Bernadotte and the UN became convinced the newly formed government of Israel would negotiate from a position of fear. Just as Golda Meir had informed King Abdullah of Jordan: the Jews would fight—and they would win!

Neither party with which Bernadotte attempted to negotiate was accepting of the UN partition plan, nor did the Palestinians seem perfectly willing to consent to Transjordan rule rather than self-government. One faction in particular, LEHI, a Jewish underground group, saw the negotiator's attempts as a major threat. LEHI leaders saw Bernadotte as a British agent and Nazi sympathizer. He was, in their eyes, a threat to Jewish independence. As a result, Commander Jehoshua Zeitler began a training program to ready assassins for the murder of Bernadotte. The decision was made to attempt the assassination while the negotiator was set to meet with Dov Joseph, Jerusalem's military governor. According to one account:

> Bernadotte's appointment with Joseph was rescheduled for 6:30 p.m. [on either September 17 or 18, 1948] . . . Bernadotte spent time at the official UN headquarters at the YMCA and at Government House, a potential headquarters for a UN mission. He visited the Jerusalem Agricultural School where he picked up French UN observer Andre Seraut who took the center seat in the UN car, immediately to Bernadotte's left. The three car convoy then headed back to the YMCA to pick up a copy of the truce regulations before the meeting with Joseph.
>
> Meanwhile, LEHI terrorists adapted their plans to the new meeting time and an Israeli military jeep carrying a driver named Meshulam Makover and four assassins was dispatched to Palmeh Street in the Jerusalem

neighborhood of Old Katamon. At 5:03 p.m., the UN convoy drove up and found the jeep blocking its path. The terrorists, wearing khaki shorts and peaked caps, left their jeep, found Bernadotte in the second car of the convoy and one man, later discovered to be Yehoshua Cohen, fired a Schmeisser automatic pistol into the car, spraying the interior with bullets and killing Seraut and then Bernadotte. . . . Both Seraut and Bernadotte were transported to Hadassah Hospital on Mount Scopus, but were found to have died instantly. [44]

Despite the US arms embargo imposed on both sides of the conflict, the Arab League had little difficulty obtaining arms from the British. It was not even a well-kept secret that Royal Air Force planes took to the skies alongside Egyptian squadrons. Four RAF planes were shot down by Israeli planes on January 7, 1949. [45]

Shortsighted Arab negotiators opted for aggression rather than compromise. By the war's end, the Arabs held even less territory than offered by Bernadotte and his UN successor, Ralph Bunche.

The Jews, backs to the wall, outgunned and outmanned, won their hard-fought independence at a terrible price. According to author and historian Howard Sachar:

> Many of its most productive [agricultural] fields
> lay gutted and mined. Its citrus groves, for decades the

basis of the Yishuv's [Jewish community] economy, were largely destroyed. [46]

The cost to protect their land and its inhabitants cost the Israelis over $500 million and approximately one percent of its population at that time—6,373 men, women and children. How many lives might have been saved had the United States and its Western Allies sufficiently armed the Jews so that they were able to protect their land and people.

During the first months of 1949, direct negotiations were conducted under UN auspices between Israel and each of the invading countries (except Iraq, which refused to negotiate with Israel), resulting in armistice agreements that reflected the situation at the end of the fighting.

Accordingly, the Coastal Plain, Galilee, and the entire Negev were within Israel's sovereignty; Judea and Samaria (the West Bank) came under Jordanian rule; the Gaza Strip came under Egyptian administration, and the city of Jerusalem was divided, with Jordan controlling the eastern part, including the Old City, and Israel the western sector. Once again, the Jews were denied access to any part of the Temple Mount.

Only through the grace and protection of God were the Jews able to survive. Again and again over the years this tiny island of freedom in the Middle East has suffered similar assaults directed by evil men dedicated to the annihilation of the Jewish people.

After the 1948 Armistice was declared between Israel and Jordan, it was thought that Jerusalem was permanently divided:

> Barbed wire and concrete barriers ran down the center of the city, passing close by Jaffa Gate on the western side of the old walled city, and a crossing point was established at Mandelbaum Gate slightly to the north of the old walled city.[47]

The Armistice provided for Israeli access to two important Jordanian-controlled areas of Jerusalem: Mount Scopus, where the campus of Hebrew University and Hadassah Hospital were located, and the Western Wall and synagogues of the Old City. Actually, the only good to come from this agreement was that the Jews were allowed to maintain a police outpost on Mount Scopus. Simon Montefiore wrote of the duplicity surrounding the division of Jerusalem under the Armistice:

> The Armistice, signed in April 1949 and supervised by the UN, who were based in the British Government House, divided Jerusalem: Israel received the west with an island of territory on Mount Scopus, while [Jordan's King] Abdullah kept the Old City, eastern Jerusalem and

the West Bank. The agreement promised the Jews access to the [Western] Wall, the Mount of Olives cemetery and the Kidron Valley tombs but his was never honored. Jews were not allowed to pray at the Wall for the next nineteen years, the tombstones in their cemeteries were vandalized.[48]

Under the UN mandate, all government services housed in East Jerusalem during the British Mandate had been transferred to Amman. Jordan's King Abdullah annexed the city and the West Bank, and the hill country of Samaria and Judea that lies north and south of Jerusalem. He then changed the name of his country from the Emirate of Transjordan to the Hashemite Kingdom of Jordan. East Jerusalem was heralded the "second capital" of Jordan, although it meant little in actual practice. The city was cut off from access to the Mediterranean and more than somewhat isolated up in the hills.

For several years following the armistice, East Jerusalem was without electricity, and water was continually in short supply. The economy was based on tourism and institutions devoted to religious research. Its only significant manufacturing facility was a lone cigarette plant. Under Jordanian oversight, building projects were nearly nonexistent, confined to a handful of hotels, churches, and hospitals.

On the other side of the wall separating Israeli and Jordanian oversight, the times were very different. The Israelis were much more aggressive in their allotted portion of Jerusalem, even though it was situated at the end of a long corridor and surrounded by hostile Arabs. Larger water pipelines replaced circa 1948 conduits, and an immense water reservoir was constructed south of the city. The already-functioning electrical network was connected to the national grid, and train service in and out of the city resumed in May 1949.

Major highway construction and other building projects were brought online quickly. Both Hadassah Medical Center and Hebrew University required new campuses to replace the facilities on Mount Scopus, which sat vacant. The complex multiplied to include a medical school, a training school for nurses, a dental school, and a wide range of specialty clinics.

The university added a stadium, synagogue, planetarium, and a major national library. A convention center for concerts, dramatic performances, exhibitions, and conferences was erected on the western outskirts of the city. In 1951 the Twenty-third Zionist Congress assembled in the center. It was the first to be held in Israel.

To the southwest of Jerusalem, Mount Herzl was turned into a national memorial park in honor of Theodor Herzl's work. Since then, many noted Zionists and Israeli leaders have been honored with burial there.

It should be noted that the establishment of the new nation of Israel in 1948 and the subsequent emigration of Jews from more than one hundred nations to populate the Jewish state has exactly fulfilled Ezekiel's prophecy in chapter thirty-six.

During a private conversation before he became prime minister of Israel, Benjamin Netanyahu once said to me:

> The truth of the matter is that if it had not been for the prophetic promises about returning to our homeland, the Jewish people would not have survived. There is something about reading the statements of the prophets in the original Hebrew language—the powerful impact of those words bore deep into your heart and is implanted in your mind. There is absolutely no question but that those ancient prophetic promises kept hope alive in the hearts of Jewish people and sustained us over the generations when we had nothing else to cling to.

From the beginning of her independence—while still at war—Israel threw open her doors to Jewish refugees. Within the first four months of that independence, some fifty thousand Jews fled to Israel—most of them Holocaust survivors. Within the first three years the total number of immigrants escalated to almost seven hundred thousand, doubling Israel's population.

In 1950 the Knesset unanimously passed the Law of Return, which states:

> 1. Every Jew has the right to come to this country as an oleh [immigrant to Israel].

> *Oleh's visa*

> 2. (a) Aliyah shall be by oleh's visa.
>
>   (b) An oleh's visa shall be granted to every Jew who has expressed his desire to settle in Israel, unless the Minister of Immigration is satisfied that the applicant
>
>   (1) is engaged in an activity directed against the Jewish people; or
>
>   (2) is likely to endanger public health or the security of the State. [49]

Over 2.5 million men, women, and children from the four corners of the earth did just that: settle in a land they had never seen, but for which they had always longed. The cry, "Next year in Jerusalem!" became a reality for them. The nation of Israel has gone to great expense to help them get there; sometimes putting together massive airlifts of thousands of Jews at a time, sometimes taking them out of hostile countries during war situations. The logistics of those airlifts was staggering, but the Israelis quickly mastered the process.

The first major airlift, in 1950, was dubbed Operation Magic

Carpet. The entire Jewish population of the Arab country of Yemen was airlifted to Israel. That was followed by the transportation of over fifty-thousand Jews from Baghdad. A tight deadline had been set by the Iraqi government before immigration to Israel became a capital offense.

Two more airlifts brought Jews, believed to have existed in Ethiopia since the time of Solomon, to a new home in Israel. Operations Moses and Joshua in 1984–1985 moved 7,500 Ethiopian Jews to Israel. When they arrived, most of them only knew two words in Hebrew: *Yerushalayim* and *shalom*—"Jerusalem" and the word of greeting that means "peace."

When civil war again broke out in the African nation in 1991, thousands more Jews were stranded. After months of difficult negotiations, and with the assistance of the United States, permission to rescue the remaining Ethiopian Jews was given. Incredibly, in less than thirty-six hours the Israeli Air Force completed Operation Solomon. A total of 14,324 men, women and children were rescued from Addis Ababa and flown to Tel Aviv before the news was leaked to the press.[50]

The largest and most prophetically significant group of immigrants came to Israel from the former Soviet Union. Approximately 100,000 Jews were allowed to emigrate in the 1970s. Many had waited years to receive exit visas, and with the collapse of Communism, the floodgates opened:

Soviet Jews were permitted to leave the Soviet Union in unprecedented numbers in the late 1980s, with President Gorbachev's bid to liberalize the country. The collapse of the Soviet Union in late 1991 facilitated this process. After 190,000 *olim* [immigrants] reached Israel in 1990 and 150,000 in 1991, the stabilization of conditions in the former Soviet Union and adjustment difficulties in Israel caused immigration to level off at approximately 70,000 per year. From 1989 to the end of 2003, more than 950,000 Jews from the former Soviet Union had made their home in Israel. [51]

Even though Israel's Ministry of Absorption was a great help in integrating the new arrivals into Israeli society, today it remains a tremendous economic burden on the Jewish state. However, the government of Israel is determined to provide a haven for Jews from any corner of the world. Despite being surrounded by hostile Arab countries, and subjected to political pressure from the West, the *raison d'etre* for the State of Israel is to continue to provide safety from any future Holocaust. For that purpose, her doors will never be closed to any Jew seeking to make *aliyah*—aka, "going up to Jerusalem."

10

THE MIDDLE EAST of the 1950s quickly became the chessboard in the Cold War. Independence was wrested from imperial powers, and Arabs began to adopt self-rule rather than British protectorate status. Two trends began in the Middle East: one toward Arab nationalism and modernization following the vision of Egyptian president Gamal Abdel Nasser; the other toward the nostalgic *Wahhabi* vision of the monarchies of the region. Saudi Arabia, of course, was the leader of this latter group. The monarchies of Saudi Arabia, Iraq, Iran, and Kuwait also had an unquestionable edge over the nationalists simply because they controlled the oil. The Cold War further polarized the region. Because of the influence of American oil companies, the United States supported the monarchies, and though both presidents Eisenhower and Kennedy made solid efforts to court Nasser, Egypt and Syria moved to the Soviet side of the table, having received most of their military technology from the Communists.

Thus the chess pieces began to be moved across the board as East and West played their game: Britain signed the Baghdad Pact in 1955 with Iraq, Iran, Turkey, and Pakistan in an attempt to keep these nations pro-Western. In 1956, Britain joined with France and Israel to invade the Sinai Peninsula, which precipitated the Suez Crisis.

On July 26, 1956, the administration of US president Dwight Eisenhower withdrew funds designated for the erection of the Aswan Dam in Egypt. Incensed by that move, Nasser proceeded to nationalize the Suez Canal, which connects the Mediterranean and Red seas. Thus, months of futile talks with the Egyptian hierarchy began in an attempt to restore international oversight for the canal. Britain then made plans with France to invade the Sinai Peninsula. The French were adamant that Israel join in the military endeavor. Shimon Peres, former prime minister and president of Israel, had worked closely to develop close ties with the French. In a meeting with the minister of defense, Maurice Bourgès-Maunoury, Peres recalled that the minister asked,

> "How much time do you reckon it would take your army to cross the Sinai Peninsula and reach Suez?" I replied that our army people estimated it would probably take from five to seven days. . . .
>
> Bourgès-Manoury [sic] "was somewhat amazed by this answer."[52]

Peres further explained that any participation by Israel would target freeing the Straits of Tiran and liberating Eilat. As Nasser's hate-filled speeches targeted the Israelis more and more, Peres returned to Paris for another meeting with the defense minister. Not only had their concern been about freeing the Straits and Eilat, but the Egyptian blockade had halted ships from reaching the ports of Haifa and Tel Aviv. Peres knew that of the countries willing to go to war to regain control of the canal, Israel had the most to lose in what was the possibility of becoming an all-out confrontation with Egypt.

Nasser's actions took the entire world by surprise; especially British and French stockholders of the Suez Canal Company. Leaders in Britain and France immediately began to make plans to wrest the canal from Nasser. The seizure of the area surrounding the Suez Canal was of great concern to Israel as well, because under Egyptian control it would have been impossible to ship goods through the Arab-controlled locale. Joining with Britain and France in what became known as the "tripartite collusion," Israel attacked the Egyptians across the Suez on October 26, which allowed the other two countries to join the battle on Israel's side.

When the Russians became involved in support of Egypt and issued threats to Britain, France, and Israel, President Eisenhower laconically responded with, "If those fellows start something, we may have to hit 'em—and, if necessary, with everything in the bucket." [53]

Backed by the Soviets and buoyed with arms shipments from the Soviet Union, Nasser ramped up his fiery speeches. He backed his rhetoric with incursions into Israel and a general disruption. Peres wrote in his journal: "This escalation of sabotage and reprisal brought the Middle East—or so it seemed to the Israelis to the edge of full-scale war, and the question seemed to be not if but when."[54]

The question was answered on Monday, October 29. Israeli pilots climbed into the cockpits of their P-51 Mustang fighters; their destination: the Sinai. Those daring men in their flying machines skimmed across the sands at an inconceivable altitude of, at times, a mere twelve feet. Their mission was to render inoperable the telephone lines that connected the Egyptian military units in the Sinai with headquarters in Cairo. They succeeded, and just hours later Israeli paratroopers boarded planes headed toward Egypt. Their destination was the Mitla Pass, just forty-five miles from the canal.

Egypt retaliated by firing rounds into Haifa from the frigate *Ibrahim al-Awal* sitting just offshore. Two Israeli destroyers—the *Jaffa* and the *Eilat*—opened fire on the frigate with air support from two French-made Israeli fighters. With no way of escape open, the captain of the *Ibrahim al-Awal* ran up a white flag and surrendered to the Israelis. The Egyptian ship was towed into the harbor at Haifa.

Although sporadic air support came from the French and British, Israel was left alone to fight the ground war against Egypt. Israel captured Egyptian fortifications at Abu Ageila, giving the Israelis a clear field to provide supplies to troops in the Sinai. With the Egyptians clearly outmaneuvered in other positions, the Syrians notified US leaders that they would join the fray. They and the Jordanians placed their troops under the command of General Abdel Hakim Amer, Egypt's chief of staff.

The Egyptian air war was generally ineffective. Shimon Peres described it thus:

> On several occasions, their [Russian-made] Ilyushin bombers penetrated Israel air space, but their pilots for the most part jettisoned their bombs on open fields where they ran no danger of counter-fire from harmless blades of grass. In each case, Cairo Radio announced that the targets—giving the names of the cities—had been attacked, just as they kept claiming "successes" and "victories" throughout the campaign.[55]

November 2 dawned with the Israelis having captured Al-Arish. By midday, the Egyptian leader in Gaza had surrendered to Israel, and IDF troops were approximately ten miles from the Suez Canal. By nightfall, UN Secretary-General Dag Hammerskjöld had proposed a cease-fire, which Israel accepted. Tellingly, among the massive stores of war materiel captured by the IDF was an item considered standard issue for Egyptian commanders: a two-volume Arabic paperback edition of Adolf Hitler's *Mein Kampf*.

When the sand had settled, the Israelis had expended only one hundred hours of fighting in order to reach their goals. They held the Gaza Strip and Sharm el-Sheikh on the Red Sea. Sadly, 231 IDF soldiers had lost their lives in the battle.

Canadian external affairs minister Lester Pearson brought a bit of sanity to bear on the parties involved. He suggested the formation of a United Nations Emergency Force to be sent to Egypt to form a buffer zone between the Egyptians and their allies. During one of the meetings, and angered by the unfairness of the UN's placing all blame on Israel, Australian prime minister Robert Gordon Menzies took the group to task:

> The United Nations made Israel a victim of a double standard of belligerent rights. Egypt sought to justify her denial of passage throughout the [Suez] Canal of Israeli ships on the grounds that she was at war and had belligerent rights, and thus she had been in contempt of the United Nations for six years. Israel, having accepted the proposition that she was at war with Egypt, attacked, but was ordered out of the Gaza strip and the Sinai peninsula; and Egypt still refuses to allow her ships safe passage; I cannot believe this kind of thing is a triumph of international justice.[57]

The presence of the peacekeeping forces slowly dispelled the threat. (In 1957 the Nobel Committee awarded Canadian soldier, scholar, statesman, and diplomat Lester Pearson, with its Peace Prize because of his efforts to avoid an all-out war in the Suez region.) UN units were withdrawn in December 1956, and the canal returned to Egypt's oversight. Israel, however, remained at Sharm el-Sheikh and in Gaza.

Eisenhower had been spared military intervention, but having taken Dulles' advice, the president proceeded to alienate the pro-Israel lobby in Washington with his attempts to placate the Arabs, who had been soundly defeated by the Israelis during the Suez Crisis. The president took to the airwaves in February 1957 to demand Israel's immediate and unconditional withdrawal from Sharm el-Sheikh and Gaza. He threatened sanctions if his demands were not met. This did not endear him to the Jewish community and particularly not to I. L. Kenen, the head of the American Israel Public Affairs Committee (AIPAC). The group had achieved its goal in securing congressional backing for the fledgling State of Israel. U.S. senators and representatives had been convinced that a tough and robust Jewish state would be a safeguard against Arab expansion in the Middle East.

The members of the organization rallied to counter Dulles's influence on Eisenhower. Both the president and the secretary of state were infuriated when Ike received a letter from congressional members outlining their disagreement with his plan to implement sanctions. So upset were the two, that a plan was developed to disallow private contributions to Israel through Jewish organizations and the purchase of Israeli bonds. AIPAC leaders went straight to Congress with this ploy and were rewarded when Eisenhower was forced to drop the proposal.

Democratic Senate Majority Leader from Texas Lyndon Baines Johnson warned Dulles that coercion would not be allowed, as it would damage the genial association between Israel and the United States. Republican Minority Leader William Knowland of California joined forces with Johnson in opposing sanctions.

Eisenhower was then placed in the position of having to soothe the rightfully ruffled feathers of Prime Minister David Ben-Gurion. The president asked the prime minister to consider withdrawal and assured Ben-Gurion he would be amply rewarded for his statesmanship. So it was that:

> Israel agreed to a withdrawal from the Sinai in 1957, on the basis that a United Nations Expeditionary Force would shield Israel's southern border from attack, and that international guarantees would ensure freedom of navigation through the Straits of Tiran. Significantly, it was the failure of these guarantees and the withdrawal of UNEF that resulted in the war of 1967.[58]

In response to the Suez Crisis, Egypt and Syria formed the United Arab Republic in 1958. It would eventually be the alliance that initiated the 1967 Six-Day War and the 1973 Yom Kippur War. In response, Jordan and Iraq formed the Arab Union of Jordan and Iraq that same year, joining together their Hashemite kingdoms. Former premier of Iraq Nuri al-Said was named leader of the new venture. Nasser responded by calling upon the people, police, and military of Iraq to overthrow their pro-Western government. This resulted in the July 14, 1958, *coup d'état* that put the military in control of the country and dissolved the Arab Union. Iraq withdrew from its own Baghdad Pact in 1959.

An odd trend began to develop: The United States would favor the regressive regimes over the progressive ones. While both were dictatorships and repressive, America suddenly found herself supporting the faction that would produce terrorism and continue to return the region to the Middle Ages, not the side that would move toward modernization and a better standard of living. As the United States had depleted its own oil reserves in Oklahoma and Texas to win the Second World War, Middle Eastern oil, and particularly that from Saudi Arabia, Iran, Iraq, and Kuwait had become of great interest, if not a necessity, to keep the US economy prospering. As Americans paid richly to pump the crude to keep its economy thriving, they were unknowingly funding a growing underground movement against Israel and stability in the region.

Through it all, Saudi Arabia maintained the neutrality Ibn Saud had exhibited during World War II. After the king died in 1953, his second son, who then became King Saud, waited to see what would transpire before taking a stand. Though Saudi Arabia had no love for the fledgling Jewish state, it was more concerned at that time with its aggressive neighbors, particularly the Hashemite kingdoms of Jordan and Iraq on its northern border. Under King Saud, and despite the continual flow of oil money into the region, Saudi Arabia plunged into financial chaos. King Saud was eventually deposed and replaced by his younger brother, Faisal bin Abdul Aziz, in 1964. The Wahhabi *ulemas* (Muslim scholars trained in Islamic law) had much to do with this change in leadership, and Faisal wouldn't forget it. Saud's government had grown soft and more open; Faisal would return the country to its ultra-conservative Wahhabi roots. Faisal, whose mother died when he was six years old, was raised by his maternal grandfather. He advised the future king, "Saudi Arabia should lead the Arab world and the ideology of Wahhabism should be exported." [59]

Though Faisal's grandfather died not long after giving him this advice, apparently it was never forgotten. It also appears Faisal was more like his father, Ibn Saud, than his older brother had been. But it was the clever, behind-the-scenes Ibn Saud that came out in Faisal rather than the cutthroat invader who had retaken Mecca and Medina. He would use his influence and the power of Wahhabism, not military might, to promote Saudi interests. Saud had supplied only two Saudi brigades to help fight the Jews in their war for independence in 1948–1949, but Faisal would only supply one for the Six-Day War in 1967. The division would see no action. Saudi Arabia ultimately benefitted from Israel's victory in many ways. With Egypt embarrassed and weakened, Nasser pulled his troops from Yemen where he had hoped a *coup* would deliver the Arabia Peninsula into Pan-Arab Nationalist control. With Nasser's withdrawal, Saudi Arabia's southern border was again secure.

Nasser's Suez fiasco, however, made one thing very clear according to historian Martin Gilbert:

> After eight years of statehood, a very brief span of time indeed in the history of nations, [Israel] no longer appeared vulnerable and temporary. Its international standing improved dramatically as a result of the campaign, as did the prowess and reputation of its citizen army, the Israel Defense Forces. Israel's perceived and actual military strength became its most important asset in its dealing with the Arab world for the next ten years.[60]

January, February, and March 1967 were rife with across-the-border bombardment by Syria against the Israelis. April 7, 1967, marked the date that Israel had reached a breaking point: IDF tanks rolled into position to return fire against Syrian tanks across the border at the B'not Yaakov Bridge. Israel's air force strafed several Syrian positions before being challenged by Soviet MiG-21 fighters.

Within a matter of minutes, Israeli pilots had shot down six MiGs and chased the remaining fighters to Damascus. One of Israel's planes was shot down. The air battle resulted in charges of aggression against the Israelis. Publicly, the Soviets supported the charge, but both the Russian ambassador and the Egyptian prime minister covertly warned Syria not to provoke the Jews. The Soviets were very vocal, however, in their condemnation of Israel's reaction to hostile acts.

None of the rhetoric persuaded Fatah to halt its campaign of terrorism against Israel. Neither was Nasser persuaded to soften his stance. In June 1967, determined to stop Israel from crossing the Syrian border in an attempt to end guerilla raids on Israeli villages, Nasser sent troops to the Israeli border. Although urged by the kings of Saudi Arabia and Jordan to withdraw, Nasser marched inexorably toward war with Israel by requesting that the UN withdraw its Emergency Force of 3,400 men stationed at Gaza and Sharm el-Sheikh from the Egyptian–Israeli border.

Martin Gilbert wrote of what was considered Israel's most inadvertent military mistake leading up to the Six-Day War:

> Hoping to assert her peaceful intentions, and to calm
> the jittery atmosphere created by Arab—and Soviet—accusations of an imminent Israeli attack on Syria, she held
> her May 15 Independence Day parade without the usual

large numbers of tanks and heavy artillery . . . because Israel did not wish to exacerbate tension on the Jordanian front.

Noting the lack of heavy armour, the Egyptians at once accused Israel of having sent the "missing' tanks and other weaponry to the north. Egypt also names May 17—a mere two days away—as the day on which Israel would invade Syria. . . . May 20, the Egyptian Minister of War, Field Marshall Abdul Hakim Amer, traveled to Gaza to inspect the Egyptian troops that had replaced the United Nations contingent. Alongside the Egyptians were soldiers of the Egyptian-sponsored Palestinian Liberation Army. [61]

Threatened by this hostile action, Israel took steps to defend her citizens in what has become known as the Six-Day War. In a feat of unparalleled planning and execution, Israeli Air Force pilots had launched Operation Focus (*Mivtza Moked*). It was the brainchild of Israel's Ezer Weizman and was smoothly executed by IAF head, Major General Mordechai Hod:

On the morning of June 5, Israel launched a full-scale attack on Egypt, Jordan, and Syria. In three hours, at least 300 of Egypt's 430 combat aircraft were destroyed, many on the ground as the pilots did not have time to take off. Israeli ground forces started a lightning strike into Sinai and by June 8 had reached the Suez Canal. On that day, both sides accepted a UN Security Council call for a cease-fire. By June 11, the Arab defeat was total; Israel now held all of historic Palestine, including the Old City of Jerusalem, the West Bank, and the Gaza Strip, as well as Sinai and part of the Golan Heights of Syria.[62]

In his book *Six Days of War,* historian, author and former ambassador Michael B. Oren wrote:

> The jets dove. They approached in foursomes and attacked in pairs, each making three passes—four, if time permitted—the first bombing and the rest to strafe. Priority was to be given to destroying the runways, then to the long-range bombers that threatened Israeli cities, and then to the jet fighters, the MiG's. Last to be raided were missile, radar, and support facilities. Each sortie was to take between seven and ten minutes. With a twenty-minute return flight, an eight-minute refueling time, and ten minutes' rest for the pilot, the planes would be in action again well within an hour. During that hour, moreover, the Egyptian bases would be under almost uninterrupted attack.[63]

In six miraculous days, Israel had again claimed the West Bank, the Sinai Peninsula, site of Israel's wanderings under Moses' leadership, had wrested the tactically important Golan Heights from Syria, the Old City of Jerusalem, and the Western Wall of the Temple Mount. The prophet Zechariah wrote in Chapter 14, verse 3:

> Then the LORD will go out and fight against those nations as when he fights on a day of battle. (ESV)

The modern-day children of Israel had lived the fulfillment of prophecy. And yet, one major error can be laid at the feet of Jewish hero Moshe Dayan; in an act of appeasement, he relinquished control of the Temple Mount to the Muslims.

11

SAUDI ARABIA'S King Faisal showed no gratitude for President Nasser's move and soon found another way to undermine Israel and those Arab states that might rival his country in the Middle East. All the while, Saudi Arabia continued to maintain solid relations with the United States as oil money flowed into Faisal's coffers. Regrettably, US dollars indirectly promoted and exported Wahhabism—the doctrine of hatred for Israel and the West.

King Faisal had begun to financially support an upstart organization born on January 1, 1965, called *Fatah* (Palestine National Liberation Movement), headed by Mohammed Yasser Abdel Rahman Abdel Raouf Arafat al-Qudwa al-Husseini, an Egyptian who adopted the more easily pronounceable and remembered moniker, Yasser Arafat. Arafat liked to advertise that he was born in Jerusalem, but like many of his "facts," that assertion proved to be false: His birth certificate was legally registered in Cairo.

Fatah and brother organizations used Saudi money to destabilize Jordan, eventually forcing that country to apply its full military might to oust the resident Palestinians during Black September—the Jordanian civil war—of 1968. However, Fatah would still manage to take full control of the Nasser-created Palestine Liberation Organization (PLO) in 1969, combining several terrorist groups under one umbrella that finally settled in Jordan.

Author, journalist, and historian Paul Johnson wrote of the worldwide influence of Arab oil and terrorism ties:

> At the UN there was an extraordinary growth in Arab influence. As a result, in 1975 the General Assembly passed a resolution equating Zionism with racialism. The mufti's successor, Yasser Arafat, leader of the main Arab terror group, the Palestine Liberation Organization, was accorded head-of-government status by the UN and by numerous states hitherto friendly to Israel. There was a real danger of Israel being driven into an international ghetto occupied solely by South Africa. . . . Had the Palestinians negotiated seriously at this time, there can be little doubt that Israel would have been obliged to yield most of the West bank. But the chance was missed in favour of fruitless terrorism . . .[64]

Arafat and what would ultimately become known as the

Palestinian Authority (PA) apparently sought to muddy the political activity by using fear tactics and sheer numbers to intimidate the late king Hussein. The Palestinians were positioned to surface as an overriding power in Transjordan politics. Their very presence, had it been allowed to expand, could well have ended the Hussein monarchy. Arafat and his subordinates were determined to undermine the king while sowing seeds of empathy and support among the populace in a country rife with unrest.

Backed by Syria, Arafat and his Fatah minions soon began to slip over the border from Jordan into Israel to make their fanatic presence known by targeting Israeli sites. One of the first was in January 1965 when organization operatives tried to bomb Israel's National Water Carrier. The attempt failed. By the late 1960s, and especially following the Six-Day War in 1967, Arafat and his crew began to openly stir up trouble for King Hussein by using his country as a base of operations against Israel. In response, reciprocal raids by Israel resulted in damage to Jordanian cities. Having deemed the organization a threat, King Hussein instructed his forces to disarm the Palestinian militia groups. The move resulted in open conflict with Arafat's PLO.

In September 1970, Egyptian president Gamal Abdel Nasser died. His successor, Anwar Sadat, was determined to regain the territory lost during the Six-Day War. Through a UN intermediary, Sadat let it be known that he would sign a peace treaty with Israel if the nation agreed to withdraw to the pre-1967 boundaries. The Knesset emphatically responded that Israel would certainly not withdraw.

Sadat's plan was to cause just enough damage to alter the Israelis' decision. The leader of Syria, Hafiz al-Assad, had no such aspirations; he was determined to reclaim the Golan Heights militarily. The Syrians had launched a massive upsurge along their border with the Golan Heights, and they planned nothing short of a decisive victory. Al-Assad had another goal in mind: to establish Syria as the supreme military force among Arab countries. He was certain that with Sadat's assistance, the two allies could strike a convincing blow to tiny Israel and ensure that the West Bank and Gaza would once again be in Arab hands.

Sadat was plagued by economic ills that he thought would be allayed by a war with Israel, the nemesis of all Arabs. Author Abraham Rabinovich wrote:

> The three years since Sadat had taken office . . . were the most demoralized in Egyptian history . . . A desiccated economy added to the nation's despondency. War was a desperate option.[65]

The Egyptian people had been put to shame by the rout of their troops during the Six-Day War. If Sadat had been successful militarily, he planned to persuade the population that reforms were necessary. University students protested against Sadat, seeing war as the only way to regain respect in the region. They were upset that Egypt's President Sadat had waited so long to retaliate against the Israelis.

King Hussein of Jordan, on the other hand, was hesitant to join any coalition to attack Israel. His country had lost much in 1967, and he was afraid of further losses in another attempt. While Sadat backed the PLO in its claims to the West Bank and Gaza, King Hussein was fighting his own battles against the terrorist organization. After several hijackings, attempts to assassinate the king, and efforts to wrest the Irbid—the area with the second largest city in the Hashemite Kingdom—from Hussein, Jordanian troops expelled the PLO from the country during what became known as Black September 1970.

In the bloody fighting that followed the king's decision, terrorists murdered Major R. J. Perry, military attaché at the United States Embassy in Amman. Then they took over two hotels, the Intercontinental and the Philadelphia, and held thirty-two American and European guests hostage. The leader, George Habash, announced that his forces would kill the hostages and blow up the hotels if Jordanian troops did not retreat. An uneasy quiet ensued, but was shattered in September when King Hussein reached his breaking point politically. A group of Palestinians hijacked three airplanes and ultimately landed all three in Jordanian territory:

✧ September 6: Trans World Airlines (TWA) Flight 741, en route from Frankfurt to New York, a Boeing 707 carrying 149 passengers and crew. Hijackers renamed the plane Gaza One and ordered it to the Jordanian airstrip.

✧ September 6: Swissair Flight 100 from Zurich to New York, a DC-8 with 155 passengers and crew. It was over France when hijackers seized it, rename it Haifa One, and order it to Dawson Field in Jordan.

✧ September 9: BOAC Flight 775 from Bombay to London, a VC-10, is seized while flying over Lebanon. (The British Overseas Airways Corporation is the forerunner to British Airways.) PFLP hijackers said they've seized the plane as ransom for the release of Leila Khaled, the foiled hijacker aboard the El Al plane. The BOAC plane carries 117 passengers and crew. It's allowed to land in Beirut, where it refuels, then flies to Dawson Field in Jordan to join the other two hijacked jets there. [66]

The group then held 445 hostages. Some were released, and by September 12 only fifty-four remained captive. The three jets were eventually blown up in Jordan.

On September 16, King Hussein announced a military government to restore order in Jordan, and at the same time Yasser Arafat was named head of the Palestine Liberation Army—the military arm of the Palestine Liberation Organization. The following morning the king unleashed the Bedouin Arab Legion in a full-scale operation against the PLO. Tanks demolished every building in Amman from which gunfire erupted. Before Hussein had regained control, an estimated three thousand Palestinian terrorists had been killed. PLO power in Jordan had been broken.

As the king's troops battled the PLO, Syria intervened, sending forces across Jordan's border. The Syrians greatly outnumbered Jordan in both tanks and aircraft, and when the king realized his predicament, requested that "the United States and Great Britain intervene in the war in Jordan."[67] He asked the United States, in fact, to attack Syria. Some transcripts of diplomatic communiqués show that Hussein actually requested Israeli intervention against Syria, "Please help us in any way possible."[68] The following missive sent from King Hussein pled for assistance:

> Situation deteriorating dangerously following Syrian massive invasion. I request immediate physical intervention both land and air . . . to safeguard sovereignty, territorial integrity and independence of Jordan. Immediate air strikes on invading forces from any quarter plus air cover are imperative.[69]

Israel and the United States mobilized forces, giving notice to

Syria that if a full-scale invasion were launched Syria would encounter more than Jordanian troops. It worked. Syria retreated, and the Jordanians were able to drive the Palestinians out.

From Jordan, the PLO moved to Lebanon, the only Arab nation with a significant Christian (Syrian Orthodox and Catholic) population. When the French pulled out of Syria and Lebanon in 1946, the Christian majority in Lebanon worked out a delicately balanced arrangement with the Muslim minority under a democratic constitution. Under that new governance Beirut became a bustling and prosperous commercial center. At that time, its citizens enjoyed the highest per capita income in the Middle East.

After Israel had become a state in 1948, several thousand Palestinian Arabs were admitted to Lebanon—not more, lest the Christian–Muslim balance of population shift disastrously. Disturbing the balance was always a matter of grave concern to the Christians who stood to lose the most.

The Palestinians, however, did disturb the balance in Lebanon—far out of proportion to their actual numbers. PLO agents worked actively inside refugee camps to establish bases from which to launch terrorist attacks on Israel. The Lebanese government was faced with a serious dilemma: If the PLO were driven out, it would anger the Muslim population; to let them stay would enrage Lebanese Christians. The prime minister began a delicate tightrope walk—he denied the existence of the PLO in public while covertly negotiating with Arafat to limit raids on Israel. His aim was to not provoke Israeli retaliation against PLO terrorists entrenched in Lebanon.

The arrangement worked only briefly. The PLO in Lebanon commandeered an Israeli El Al airliner. Israel responded by dispatching fighter jets to Beirut's airport to destroy Arab aircraft on the ground. While the Lebanese government was knocked off-balance, its Muslim neighbors pressed for the right of the PLO to supervise and police refugee camps in southern Lebanon. Additionally, PLO terrorists imprisoned for subversive activities were released from Lebanese prisons. The result: burgeoning terror activities inside Lebanon.

In September 1972, Black September, another arm of the PLO led by Mohammed Oudeh, claimed responsibility for the deaths of eleven Israeli athletes during the Munich Olympics in Germany. Members of the militant extremist group with ties to Arafat's Fatah organization had taken those eleven members hostage. After hours of negotiations between the leaders of the terrorist group and the German police, the eleven Israelis, five terrorists, and one German police officer would die during a bloody gun battle at the NATO air base in Fürstenfeldbruck. Its chief financial officer at that time was Abu Mazen (a.k.a. Mahmoud Abbas, who would later become head of the Palestinian Authority, a post he still holds today).

While Lebanon dealt with the PLO problem, Egypt's president Anwar Sadat was busily planning an attack against Israel to gain a foothold and therefore a bargaining chip to retake the lands lost in

1967. On October 24, 1972, he announced his plan to the Egyptian Supreme War Council. He also sought the assistance of Syria and Jordan. Both declined to join Egypt in an attack, as did Lebanon. Authors Simon Dunstan and Kevin Lyles wrote:

> Egypt and Syria had both lost territory in 1967 but their aims were now different. Egypt had accepted Resolution 242 and was prepared to recognize Israel while Syria was not. Moreover, Sadat's war aims were directed at the recovery of the Arab territory lost in 1967. In contrast, Syria, in common with the Palestine Liberation Organization (PLO) which it harbored, was bent on Israel's destruction.[70]

Undeterred, Sadat made a diplomatic push to engage support for his plan. By late 1973, he had been joined by approximately one hundred states within Arab countries and had enticed several European nations into joining Arabs on the UN Security Council in unifying for an offensive against Israel.

In May 1973, a 4,000-year-old nation celebrated a twenty-fifth anniversary. The Israelis expressed their pride in their age-old heritage while enjoying the newness of their independence. It was quite the paradox—old, yet new. After the rout during the 1967 war, Israel was confident that another war was unlikely. With that in mind, the IDF requested a budget that would cover only a five- or six-day battle.

A false alarm in mid-1973 was aroused by an Egyptian high probability alert. The Israel Defense Forces was not particularly alarmed and its leaders decided to lessen the number of months of mandatory service for recruits. Defense spending dropped and Minister of Defense Moshe Dayan made light of a warning from air force general Benjamin Peled. Peled thought that in the event of an impending war, a preemptive strike was absolutely necessary. This response served to dampen any sense of approaching peril.

September 13, 1973, was a further catalyst for the Arab world, but it was still not alarming for Israel. On that date, Syrian fighter jets clashed with Israeli aircraft. Thirteen Syrian planes were downed, and only one Israeli Air Force jet was lost. When the Syrians began to amass troops on the Golan Heights, it was thought to be simply saber rattling in response to the massive air-power loss. This would be a deadly miscalculation for Israel.

12

AT 2:00 P.M. on October 6, 1973, Yom Kippur, the holiest day of the Jewish year, air raid sirens broke the solemnity of the afternoon. Israel was tragically caught off-guard. Most of the members of its citizen army were in synagogues, its national radio was off the air, and people were enjoying a restful day of reflection and prayer. Therefore, Israel had no immediate response to the coordinated attacks. Israeli intelligence had not seen the assault coming, and her military was ill prepared to retaliate.

The Arab coalition had launched the sneak attack against Israel in the hope of finally driving the Jews into the Mediterranean. Shortly after the raucous noise of sirens penetrated the airwaves, Israeli radio broke with tradition and alerted its citizens that the nation was under siege. Egyptian forces were moving across the Suez Canal, and Syrian troops were crossing the Golan Heights. Israel's 200,000 reserve troops would be faced with a heart-stopping number of Egyptian and

Syrian soldiers—300,000 from Syria, 850,000-plus from Egypt. Israel's forces were outnumbered by approximately six to one.

As morning broke on October 7, Israel's nearly three hundred tanks had been reduced to about one hundred in operation. Two more divisions were mobilized, one under the command of Major General Ariel Sharon, the other commanded by Major General Avraham Adan. Minister of Defense Moshe Dayan suggested a retreat to the Mitla and the Gidi passes. He believed these to be more defensible locations. Army chief of staff General David Elazar disagreed. He thought a site nearer the canal would provide a better spot from which to launch a counterattack. Even as he and Dayan debated the possibilities, the bloody and deadly battle raged.

While every available individual was engaged in fighting, Australian Jews arrived in Israel to supplement civilian jobs. Over $100 million was sent to Israel by American Jews. On the other side of the battle lines, Algerians and Moroccans volunteered to fight against Israel.

As Egypt attacked across the Suez Canal, the battle raged for three days before the Egyptian army established entrenchments, which resulted in an impasse. On the northern border, Syria also launched an offensive. The initial assault was successful but quickly lost momentum. By the third day of fighting, Israel had lost several thousand soldiers (more Israeli causalities were lost on the first day than in the entire Six-Day War), forty-nine planes, one-third (more than five hundred) of her tank force, and a good chunk of the buffer lands gained in the Six-Day War. The Israelis seemed to again be on the brink of a holocaust.

On the fourth day of the war, in an act of desperation, the indomitable Prime Minister Golda Meir reportedly opened up three nuclear silos and pointed the missiles toward Egyptian and Syrian military headquarters near Cairo and Damascus. Army chief of staff Moshe Dayan was said to be prepared to announce to the media what he referred to as "the end of the Third Temple." The announcement was forbidden by Prime Minister Meir. Later Dayan told the press, "The situation is desperate. Everything is lost. We must withdraw."[71] So alarmed was Prime Miniser Meir that she appointed General Aharon Yariv as press spokesperson. When he delivered the press briefing on October 8, Yariv quipped, "And now ladies and gentlemen, the Syrians have fired, the Egyptians have fired, we have fired, and now you fire."[72] His statement was in hopes that the press would call the world's attention to Israel's plight.

By the morning of October 10, after days of fierce fighting, Syria had been pushed back to the line near the Golan Heights from which they had originally launched their offensive. General Elazar persuaded Meir to push farther into Syria to provide a clear path to launch artillery fire into Damascus to deter the Syrians from renewing their efforts. That evening at 8:30 p.m., a subdued and bitter Meir addressed the nation. She declared, "Everything that is in the hands of the Syrian and Egyptian soldier, all this comes from the Soviet Union."[73]

Twenty-four hours after the prime minister had made her declaration, eighty Soviet planes loaded with war materiel sat on Syrian runways. Iraqi troops numbering approximately 15,000 had reached the Syrian front. Meanwhile on the Canal front, the Israelis were holding their own against Egyptian tank battalions. At day's end, the Egyptians had lost 264 tanks, the Israelis ten. On the Syrian front, an Iraqi brigade was totally decimated and eighty tanks destroyed. An Israeli commando unit had destroyed the only bridge that would have allowed reinforcements to reach the Iraqis.

In the United States at that time, Richard Nixon occupied the Oval Office. Earlier in his presidency, "Nixon made it clear he believed warfare was inevitable in the Middle East, a war that could spread and precipitate World War III, with the United States and the Soviet Union squaring off against each other."[74] The president was now staring down the barrel of that war; he authorized Henry Kissinger to put every American plane that could fly in the air to transport all available conventional arms to Israel. The amount of materiel needed to defend Israel was more than the supplies airlifted to Berlin following World War II; it literally turned the tide of the war, saving Israel from extermination and the world from a possible nuclear conflagration. Nixon carried President Kennedy's agreement to militarily support Israel to the next logical level—a full military alliance.

The IDF launched a counteroffensive within the week and drove the Syrians to within twenty-five miles of Damascus. Attempting to aid the Syrians, the Egyptian army went on the offensive, all to no avail. Israeli troops crossed the Suez Canal and encircled the Egyptian Third Army. When the Soviets realized what was happening, they scrambled to further assist Egypt and Syria. The Soviet threat was so real Nixon feared direct conflict with the USSR and elevated all military personnel worldwide to DefCon III, meaning forces should prepare for the likelihood of war. However, on October 24 a cease-fire was finally worked out between the United States and the USSR, adopted by all parties involved, and the Yom Kippur War had mercifully ended.

Paul Johnson stated a very practical fact in *A History of the Jews*:

> Israel's willingness to accept a cease-fire was dictated more by political and psychological than by military factors. In each of the four wars there was a complete lack of symmetry. The Arab countries could afford to lose many wars. Israel could not afford to lose one. An Israeli victory could not win peace. But an Israeli defeat meant catastrophe.[75]

Nixon left office under a swirling cloud of darkness following the eruption of the Watergate scandal, which exploded due to the June 1972 break-in and burglary of the Watergate complex in Washington, D.C. The attempted cover-up by the president elicited threats of a Senate trial. On August 8, 1974, Nixon, accompanied by his family, made a television appearance to announce that he would resign his office and relinquish duties to Vice President Gerald Ford. A month later the Nixon family returned to San Clemente, California, and President Ford issued a "full, free, and absolute pardon."[76] When the dust from the debacle had settled, forty-three people had been tried, convicted, and imprisoned—many of them Nixon's top aides.

Despite his exile from politics, Nixon was ultimately viewed as an elder statesman, his advice enthusiastically sought. On April 18, 1994, Richard Milhous Nixon suffered a severe stroke and died four days later. He was buried on the grounds of the Nixon Library in Yorba Linda, California. History has been somewhat kind to the former president, but perhaps his greatest accolade came from Prime Minister Golda Meir:

> However history judges Richard Nixon—and it is probable that the verdict will be very harsh—it must also be put on the record forever that he did not break a single one of the promises he made to us.[77]

It was shortly after this, in 1974, that US leaders finally decided to give normal military aid to Israel for the first time. If Israel were attacked again, the United States pledged to do whatever was necessary to protect her as a full ally. If a strong Israel could deter another possible war or even defend herself if necessary, it would save higher direct expenditures in the long run.

Congress voted for first-aid packages to Israel with parts earmarked for defense. Before this time, most aid to Israel had been in the form of loans, all of which Israel has repaid. There were some loans made for defense reasons, but no grants or gifts. Starting in 1976, however, Israel would become the largest recipient of United States foreign assistance. Since 1974, Israel has received several billions in aid, much of those in loans. Israel has been continuously surrounded by enemies since the rebirth of the nation in 1948, but at least for a while she has found a strong ally in the United States.

13

AFTER THE OCTOBER 1973 war between Arab countries and Israel, Yasser Arafat opted to take a different approach: The despot decided to become a diplomat. With the use of smoke and mirrors and sleight of hand, the newly made-over terrorist managed to create the illusion of civility and legitimacy. With dogged determination, he gained acceptance as the leader of the PLO pack.

His transformation obviously did not deflect his determination to destroy Israel in whatever way he deemed appropriate. Arafat and his Palestine Liberation Organization, as well as other self-styled terrorist groups, failed to bolster the position of the Palestinian people by continuing attacks against the Israelis at home and abroad:

✦ March 2, 1973: PLO terrorists murdered Cleo Noel, US Ambassador to the Sudan, and his chargé d'affaires, George Moore. The terrorists were arrested but for some unknown reason were not charged with the murders—even though proof pointed directly at Arafat as a party in the crime.

✧ February 1978: A bomb planted on a bus filled to capacity exploded in Jerusalem; two were murdered, forty-six injured.

✧ March 11, 1978: A Fatah terrorist murdered Gail Rubin, niece of U.S. Senator Abraham Ribicoff, on a Tel Aviv beach.

✧ March 11, 1978: PLO terrorists seized a bus on the coastal road, killing thirty-five men, women, and children.

✧ March 17, 1978: PLO terrorists launched Katuysha rockets on the Western Galilee, killing two and wounding two.

✧ June 2, 1978: A PLO terrorist bombed a Jerusalem bus, killing six and wounding nineteen.

✧ August 20, 1978: PLO terrorists attacked Israel's El Al airlines crew members in London airport, killing a stewardess and wounding eight.

✧ December 21, 1978: PLO terrorists launched a Katuysha rocket, killing one and wounding ten in Kiryat Shmona.[78]

Of course, the infamous events surrounding the 1976 raid on Entebbe cannot be omitted. It was during this rescue mission that Prime Minister Benjamin Netanyahu's brother, Jonathan, became the only casualty. Paul Johnson wrote:

> The age of international terrorism, created by post-war Soviet-Arab anti-Semitism, effectively opened in 1968 when the Palestine Liberation Organization formally adopted terror and mass murder as its primary policy. The PLO, and its various competitors and imitators, directed their attacks primarily against Israeli targets but they made no attempt to distinguish between Israeli citizens, or Zionists, and Jews, any more than traditional anti-Semitic killers distinguished between religious Jews and Jews by birth. When members of the Baader-Meinhof gang, a German fascist left organization inspired by Soviet anti-Semitic propaganda, hijacked and Air France aircraft flying from Paris to Tel Aviv on 27 June 1976, and forced it to land in Idi Amin's Uganda, the terrorists carefully separated the non-Jews from the Jews, who were taken aside to be murdered. One of those they planned to kill still had the SS concentration camp number tattooed on his right arm.
>
> Terrorism on the scale and of the sophistication

employed by the PLO was a menacing novelty. But to the Jews there was nothing new in the principle of terrorism. For terror had been used against Jews for 1,500 years or more.[79]

The killing did not end when the clock struck midnight December 31, 1978. Arafat's *intifadas* against Israel have continued to produced death and destruction from then until now. Many fail to comprehend what it is like to live in a city so vulnerable to the violence of terror attacks. Journalist David Grossman describes it this way:

> An international TV program once interviewed a young Israeli couple and asked how many children they wanted to have. The beautiful bride said immediately: "Three." And the interviewer asked: "Why three?" And she said with a smile: "So that if one of them is killed in a war or in terror we shall still have two left."
>
> We did not have three children out of this calculation, but I must admit that this thought had crossed my mind when we started having children. The option of personal catastrophe is connected to the special fate of this country.
>
> As I fear for my children, all my life I lived with this fear of what happens if a catastrophe occurs in Israel. The question of whether we shall exist here in the future,

whether we will still live here within a few decades time, prevails subconsciously in the mind of most Israelis. We are living with difficult and partly violent neighbors, most of whom don't want us here. Some of them even threaten to eradicate us. I take them very seriously.[80]

Jerusalemites perpetually live under the threat of death, where everyday decisions often evolve into crucial situations. Their city has been repeatedly ransacked, captured, or faced major sieges.

With the perils and complexities of Jerusalem's stormy past and continued threats to her security, keep in mind that this is not just a story of kings and soldiers and armies. It is that of civilians—men like David Grossman and his family—who are the ones to pay the heaviest price for living in this city threatened constantly by turbulence of one kind or another.

Despite Arafat's fingerprints being all over attacks within Israel's borders, his good friend and confidant President Jimmy Carter continued to provide help. His pro-Arafat and pro-Palestinian leanings are legendary. According to Carter's assessment in his book *Palestine: Peace Not Apartheid* (one, I might add, that seems to be held by the world at large), Israel is the crux of the problem. Never mind that Israel has endured decades of terror attacks from the PA, Lebanon, Syria, and Gaza, worthless peace agreements, and a desire by its Arab neighbors to see it "wiped off the map." In the eyes of many, Arafat was the poor, pitiful, put-upon Palestinian leader sorely abused by the Israelis.

By 1994, Arafat had risen in notoriety to lead the Palestinian Authority that had emerged as a result of the Oslo Accords. In 1996, he was elected president of the organization by an overwhelming 83 percent. He served in that position three years before his death.

By the time William Jefferson Clinton assumed office as the 42ⁿᵈ president of the United States, Yasser Arafat was a household name everywhere and had become a major player in the Middle Eastern version of Russian roulette. One can only wonder how a fanatical terrorist like Arafat could achieve the position of viable "peace partner" with Israel. Perhaps the answer can be found in advice that Arafat received from heinous Romanian dictator Nicolae Ceauşescu:

> In the shadow of your government-in-exile [PLO], you can keep as many operational groups as you want, as long as they are not publicly connected with your name. They could mount endless operations all around the world, while your name and your 'government' would remain pristine and unspoiled, ready for negotiations and further recognition. [81]

President Clinton, working with Israel's prime minister Ehud Barak, was determined to put together the same kind of peace agreement that had been set in motion by Carter and the then- prime minister Menachem Begin at Camp David in 1978. That attempt had resulted in a treaty between Israel and Egypt. The president was determined to fashion a workable plan even though Arafat had done little since Oslo to convince Israel he was willing to compromise. Conversely, Arafat seemed resolute in his dream to destroy the Jewish nation. Despite that, Barak was willing to sit down and agree to most of the Palestinian's demands: withdrawal from 97 percent of the West Bank and 100 percent of the Gaza Strip; destruction of many of the settlements; creation of a Palestinian state with East Jerusalem as its capital.

Arafat was required only to acknowledge that Israel was a sovereign state, allow control of the Western Wall, and permit three Israeli-manned early-warning stations in the Jordan Valley. Arrogantly, Arafat walked away from the negotiating table and launched still another intifada against Israel.

Terrorists, emboldened by Arafat's refusal to cooperate, targeted unsuspecting Israelis with suicide bombings, and opened fire on buses, shopping malls, restaurants, and other locations. Victims were murdered or maimed with impunity. Families were torn apart, children orphaned, parents left childless in the wake of terrorism that ran rampant through the cities of Israel. The more Arafat was warned to cease his terror activities, the more determined he seemed to be to escalate them. And yet, the ranks of such organizations—Fatah,

Hezbollah, Hamas, Islamic Jihad, ISIS, and others—continue to swell long after the death of their role model.

Arafat succumbed to "flu-like" symptoms in 2004, after having been transported to Paris, France, for treatments. An autopsy that could have revealed the cause of death was refused by his widow, Suha. In 2005, medical records were opened, disclosing that the PA leader had died from a possible stroke. After a review of the records, some analysts suggest Arafat may have died from AIDS.

Adam and Eve in the garden of Eden learned a hard lesson that today's politicians seem determined to ignore: It is never advisable to sell one's soul to Lucifer in order to keep him at bay. Sooner or later, evil demands the ultimate sacrifice and will achieve its goals not through compromise but through terror and coercion.

The only things the Jewish people have received from repeated Palestinian negotiations have been intifadas, terrorist attacks too numerous to recount, untold numbers of civilians maimed and slaughtered, and the disdain of the world at large.

14

AFTER PLACING his signature on the Camp David Accords in 1979, Prime Minister Menachem Begin approved a massive airlift of Ethiopian Jews. Those refugees had crossed the border from Ethiopia into the Sudan where some ten thousand were stranded in refugee camps. The death toll of those who did not make it to the relative safety of a camp totaled more than two thousand. As mentioned earlier, wishing to spare further death the Israelis planned the massive airlift dubbed Operation Moses, and Operation Joshua. Chartered planes from Belgium transported some 6,500 Jews to Israel. The remaining approximately two hundred Jews in the Sudan were aided in their escape by the US Central Intelligence Agency in an airlift named Operation Sheba. Between 1972 and 1985, thousands of Ethiopian Jews were resettled in Israel, many having never experienced running water or electricity. [82]

June 1981 revealed yet another audacious decision by Begin. In a completely clandestine move, he ordered an attack on Iraq's nuclear facilities. The fledgling program, begun in the 1960s, had languished until the late 70s when the purchase of a plutonium production reactor from France raised eyebrows, and the French declined the request. Leaders did agree to erect a research reactor and laboratories. Construction began on an Osiris (so named after the Egyptian god of the dead) "40-megawatt light-water reactor," which was renamed Osiraq (or Osirik) in an attempt to include the name of the country.

Fully comprehending the seriousness of a nuclear reactor in the hands of Saddam Hussein and his plan to acquire nuclear weapons, the Israelis worked intensely to dissuade the French from completing the project in Iraq. Israel's minister of foreign affairs Yitzhak Shamir tried to reason with both Valéry Giscard d'Estaing and François Mitterrand. Shamir was unsuccessful; the French were intractable. An appeal to the Italians for assistance was similarly rebuffed. Once again, the promise of oil proved to be more important than the safety of an entire region. Although both US Secretary of Defense Caspar Weinberger and Secretary of State Alexander Haig failed to recognize the dire threat to safety, neither opted to act in Israel's favor.

Thus was born the idea of an Israeli airstrike against the reactor before it was brought online. According to Shamir, U.S. reluctance could have been caused by the fact that Iraq was embroiled in a war with Iran, an avowed enemy of the United States.[83] With diplomacy off the table, Begin moved inexorably toward the decision of a preemptive

strike against Iraq. He knew full well what one consequence would be
should the Israelis not be successful: the loss of his position as prime
minister. It was, however, a risk he was prepared to take to ensure
the security of his country and her people.

June 7, 1981, dawned with the mission having been given a green
light. Lieutenant General Rafael Eitan personally briefed the flight
crews of the fourteen F-15s and F-16s at Etzion Air Force Base in the
Negev. The men at the controls would be forced to fly at low-level
altitude through air space controlled by Jordan, Saudi Arabia, and Iraq
before reaching their target. An account of the attack was provided
by writer Yated Neeman:

> The jets roared off from Israel's giant Etzion air
> base, near Eilat, on a clear Sunday afternoon on June
> 7th at 3:00 p.m., and set off under strict radio silence.
> No one would know if the raid was a success or failure
> until the planes hopefully returned four hours later. The
> planes zoomed on a roundabout route over the north
> Saudi Arabian desert to avoid the Middle East's spider
> web of radar stations and, to be double-certain, the planes
> avoided radar by hugging the ground at treetop level....
> at 5:33 p.m., the leading pilots spotted the 60-foot reactor
> dome in the distance. The eight F-15s zoomed thousands
> of feet upwards to provide air cover while the eight F-16s

climbed a few hundred feet in preparation for exquisitely accurate bombing dives.

At 6:35 p.m. local time, the first jet's bombs smashed the reactor's concrete roof and, one after the other, with no more than fifteen seconds between them, the remaining seven planes reduced the reactor to scrap. In eighty seconds, thirteen bombs had blown away Tammuz-17's dome and demolished its reactor core. Every bomb scored a direct hit within thirty feet of the center of the target raising the mistaken theory that an electronic homing device had been planted there in advance. The pilots' speed and precision barely gave the anti-aircraft gunners a chance to react. . . . At 7:00 p.m., the first F-16 made it back to base and the rest of the planes landed in different bases within the next ten minutes. [84]

The one person who might have created havoc for Israel was vacationing in Aqaba while the attack was being carried out. Jordan's King Hussein saw the planes cruising just above the tree line and alerted the Iraqis. Apparently Iraq did not receive the king's communique, and the rest is history.

Although the United States publicly decried the attack, upon being told of the Osiraq bombing by his national security advisor, Richard V. Allen, President Ronald Reagan responded with a wink and commented, "Boys will be boys." Purdue University professor of political science and international law Louis Rene Beres wrote:

> Israel's citizens, together with Jews and Arabs, American, and other coalition soldiers who fought in the Gulf War may owe their lives to Israel's courage, skill, and foresight in June 1981. Had it not been for the brilliant raid at Osiraq, Saddam's forces might have been equipped with atomic warheads in 1991. Ironically, the Saudis, too, are in Jerusalem's debt. Had it not been for Prime Minister Begin's resolve to protect the Israeli people in 1981, Iraq's SCUDs falling on Saudi Arabia might have spawned immense casualties and lethal irradiation.[85]

The success of the attack was, perhaps, never fully apparent to the United States until 1991. During a visit to Israel in June of that year, the then-defense secretary Richard "Dick" Cheney delivered a satellite photo of the rubble that had been Osirik to Major General David Ivri, commander of the Israeli Air Force. Cheney had penned the following on the photograph: "For General David Ivri, with thanks and appreciation for the outstanding job he did on the Iraqi Nuclear Program in 1981, which made our job much easier in Desert Storm."[86]

Begin had little to fear politically after the blow dealt to Hussein's nuclear reactor. When the Israelis went to the polls on June 30, 1981, Begin's Likud Party won a total of forty-eight seats—five more than during the previous election. With the assistance of the two major religious parties, Begin was easily able to form a majority coalition. In October of that year, Begin's partner in the Camp David peace treaty with Egypt didn't fare as well. During a victory parade to celebrate Egypt's crossing of the Suez Canal in 1973, predominately Western-manufactured armaments rolled past Egyptian president Sadat's reviewing stand and Mirage jets roared over the crowd. The distractions masked the approach of Egyptian Army lieutenant Khalid al-Islambouli as he walked calmly toward the reviewing stand. As Sadat, surrounded by foreign dignitaries, rose to salute the lieutenant, members of the murderous group Egyptian Islamic Jihad began spraying the reviewing stand with assault rifles, and tossing grenades at the Egyptian leader. When the smoke from the attack had cleared, Anwar Sadat and eleven others had been slain, including the Cuban ambassador and an Omani general. Twenty-eight, including Egyptian vice president Hosni Mubarak, were wounded.

Earlier in the day, Sadat's wife, Jehan, had implored him to don a bulletproof vest for the parade. Sadat declined with, "When God is ready to take me, he'll take me." Mrs. Sadat was said to have countered, "Okay, but you don't have to help." [87]

Even as Egypt prepared for the celebration that would claim the life of Anwar Sadat, Israel was being drawn into still another war in an attempt to secure its border with Lebanon. On June 6, 1982, Beirut, Lebanon, witnessed one of the most traumatic days in its history with air, sea, and land bombardments from all sides. Israel was seeking to oust the infamous terrorist organization, the PLO, and put an end to attacks against Israeli cities in northern Israel. In a singular humanitarian act, and within minutes of the attack, pink leaflets that warned the residents to flee had been dropped from Israeli jets and littered the streets. Israel swept north to Beirut, driving the PLO northward before advancing Israeli troops. There was little bloodshed in the first three days. Most of the PLO terrorists chose to run rather than fight. The Shi'ites and Christians in southern Lebanon were celebrating. Israel was at the point of entering Beirut and rooting out the PLO once and for all, but the Arab-favoring US State Department lobbied President Reagan to stop Israel.

The Soviets had not remained strictly on the sidelines during this lethal altercation. When the IDF entered PLO trenches in Lebanon, the soldiers found extensive truckloads of war materiel. The discovery totaled "5,630 tons of ammunition; 1,320 [Soviet] armored vehicles, including . . . tanks; 1,352 anti-tank weapons; 82 artillery pieces, 215 mortars; 62 Katuysha rocket launchers; 196 anti-aircraft guns; and 33,303 small arms. These arms had been [covertly] supplied by the Soviet Union and Warsaw Pact countries, Red China, North Korea, and Vietnam."[88]

As the battle raged, the Lebanese Red Crescent (the equivalent of the American Red Cross) sent a picture of a child with limbs blown off to President Reagan. He was told that the Israelis had caused the injuries, and that a holocaust was taking place in Lebanon. Reagan was deeply moved and disturbed. It was later discovered that the picture had been fabricated. The injuries to the child were not at all the result of the Lebanese invasion.

By September, the Israelis had been joined in the fighting by Lebanese Christian Militia, a.k.a. Phalangists. On September 14, 1982, the Israeli military authorized the entrance of about 150 Phalangist militiamen into the Shatila and Sabra refugee camps. What ensued was a horrifying massacre of Shi'ite and Palestinian civilians. An investigation was ordered to determine culpability, and the conclusion was that, indeed, the soldiers under the leadership of Ariel Sharon had done nothing to stop the attack.

The Begin government survived, but the prime minister, assaulted by screams of "murderer" even during the Knesset debates, was shaken both politically and personally. Israel's struggle for safety and security had again taken a huge toll. Under tremendous pressure, Prime Minister Begin hesitated for three weeks, during which time the PLO became entrenched in Beirut.

Secretary of State Haig was extremely upset because Israel had Arafat in their crosshairs, but the United States had instructed them not to touch the PLO leader or his organization. Haig knew the PLO would eventually leave Lebanon with their rifles in their hands, and he fully supported Israel's dealing with the PLO right then.

15

IN DECEMBER 1987 Yasser Arafat and the PLO launched the *First Intifada* (or shaking off). It was a mass uprising against Israeli rule in the Palestinian territories and would continue for almost five years. The rebellion began in the Jabalia Camp (a Palestinian refugee camp) and quickly spread throughout Gaza, the West Bank, and East Jerusalem. Palestinian actions ranged from civil disobedience to open violence. In addition to general strikes, boycotts on Israeli products, graffiti and barricades, Palestinian demonstrations that included stone-throwing by youths against the Israel Defense Forces brought international attention. Conversely, the Israeli army's heavy-handed response to the demonstrations—with live ammunition, beatings, and mass arrests—garnered international condemnation. The PLO, which until then had never been recognized as leaders of the Palestinian people by Israel, would be invited to peace negotiations the following year.

Arafat was sorely disappointed by the Reagan administration in November 1988 when State Department officials declared the PLO leader would not be admitted into the United States. The reasoning behind the refusal to allow Arafat to address the United Nations was that he "knows of, condones and lends support to" acts of terrorism. To maneuver around that impasse, a proposal was offered that would move the session to a temporary site outside the United States and beyond its control. That proposal quickly gained support and on December 2 delegates voted to adjourn the General Assembly meeting in New York and reconvene in Geneva, Switzerland. Arafat was invited to deliver his address there.

Advance copies of Arafat's speech contained language deemed sufficient by the State Department to indicate acceptance of UN resolutions 242 and 338, explicit recognition of Israel's right to exist, and renunciation of terrorism—key elements in gaining US agreement to discuss the Palestinian question in direct talks with the PLO. During his delivery, however, Arafat departed from key portions of that language.

Afterward, US officials reiterated their earlier position that he had not done enough to win their participation in talks. As a result, Arafat was forced to hold a press conference to straighten things out. Chicago Tribune journalist R.C. Longworth explained how Arafat circumvented US objections:

But while Arafat was meeting the Americans, he also was negotiating with [Secretary of State George] Shultz, through Swedish Foreign Minister Sten Andersson. Shultz demanded that Arafat state clearly that he recognizes Israel's right to exist, that he renounces terrorism and that he accepts Resolutions 242 and 388, without qualifications. . . . Using Andersson as a mailbox, Arafat sent a letter to Shultz telling him what language he planned to use here. According to PLO and Swedish sources, Shultz agreed. . . . The Americans told Arafat what they wanted. They also apparently wanted it in English, not in Arabic, which can be more imprecise. . . . Arafat, whose English is uncertain, astonished reporters by reading a statement in English before answering questions in Arabic. The key part of the statement said: "In my speech . . . yesterday it was clear that we mean our people's rights to freedom and national independence according to Resolution 181, and the right of all parties concerned in the Middle East conflict to exist in peace and security—and, as I have mentioned, including the State of Palestine and Israel and other neighbors—according to Resolution 242 and 338. As for terrorism . . . I repeat for the record that we totally and absolutely renounce all forms of terrorism, including individual, group and state terrorism."

The differences were minuscule. But they were enough. The Americans bought it.[89]

Although Arafat made a big show of renouncing terrorism, the intifada entered its second year at the end of 1988. Apparently the Geneva speech so carefully crafted by the US State Department was not worth the paper on which it was written or the time necessary to fashion the statements word by word.

By decade's end, skirmishes targeting Jews were still the order of the day. Martin Gilbert wrote of one particular incident:

> Reflecting on the Arab reaction that 'the Jews are afraid', Eric Silver [British journalist for the London-based *Jewish Chronicle*] commented, 'The Jews say it is not so much fear as prudence. Why risk a knife in the back, a rock through the windscreen?' . . . On June 22, three weeks after Silver wrote those words, Professor Menachem Stern—a Hebrew University scholar and member of the Israel Academy of Arts and Sciences— was stabbed to death by two teenage Arabs. The killing took place in West Jerusalem . . . His attackers later told the police that they had killed him as an 'initiation rite', in order to qualify for membership in Yasser Arafat's Fatah. They had not known who Stern was, nor had they cared. . . . A terrorist attack, moments of tribute, sudden

deaths and the life stories of each of the victims published in every newspaper and read by the whole country, the frightened anticipation of the next bloodshed, the next account of lives cut short: these were the terrible interruptions of daily existence that marked and marred the evolution of the Jewish State in its fifth decade.[90]

The 1991 Persian Gulf War was the chink in the armor of American support for Israel. The IDF was denied the right to defend Israel during the conflict by the administration of President George H. W. Bush, yet that nation's leaders honored their word during the war with Hussein. There was no retribution for the Scuds that rained down on her. No reprisal for the threats of chemical warfare.

According to estimates, Israel paid highly for the privilege of not being permitted to defend her citizens:

> The damage caused by the 39 Iraqi Scud missiles that landed in Tel Aviv and Haifa was extensive. Approximately 3,300 apartments and other buildings were affected in the greater Tel Aviv area. Some 1,150 people who were evacuated had to be housed at a dozen hotels at a cost of $20,000 per night.
>
> Beyond the direct costs of military preparedness and damage to property, the Israeli economy was also hurt by the inability of many Israelis to work under the

emergency conditions. The economy functioned at no more than 75 percent of normal capacity during the war, resulting in a net loss to the country of $3.2 billion.

The biggest cost was in human lives. A total of 74 people died as a consequence of Scud attacks. Two died in direct hits, four from suffocation in gas masks and the rest from heart attacks.[91]

Following the conflict, Israel was ordered to Madrid, her leaders pressured to give up yet more land for peace. The conference was scheduled for October 30 through November 1, 1991.

Though with perhaps the best of intentions, the George H. W. Bush plan for peace was little more than a warmed-over version of every other plan put forward by the West, at least since the Carter administration, to solve the problem of the Palestinians. The plan again shifted the burden of peace to Israel, calling for her to give up large portions of her territory. The arrogance of the West telling Israel how to solve her problems was exasperating. None of the major powers of the world would ever allow any other country to dictate the terms of their policies. Yet they saw no problem with telling Israel the great price it must pay for a peace pleasing to nations who had not the slightest care for Israel's future.

Not only that, but much of the territory controlled by Israel was won as a result of the war initiated by the Arabs—a war that ended badly for the Palestinians. Now they wanted the lost territory back and they wanted the nations of the world to force Israel to return it. Official sessions of the conference were held at the Royal Palace, located in downtown Madrid. It was a beautiful location from an aesthetic perspective, but the glamour was little more than a façade for the actual purpose of the gathering, which was to wrest more land in Palestine from the Jews and give it to the Arabs. "Land for peace," they called it. The only problem was the Arabs didn't want peace; they wanted the Jewish inhabitants of the land pushed into the Mediterranean Sea. They wanted all of Israel and the so-called "land for peace" initiative was simply an attempt to establish new inroads into the nation of Israel.

On Friday, the final day of the conference, all heads of state were present, including President Bush and Russian president Mikhail Gorbachev. As they watched, I listened as Prime Minister Shamir stood and announced to the gathering, "I have to leave now. I am an Orthodox Jew and must return to Israel before sundown to observe Shabbat. However, I leave these proceedings in the hands of my able delegation who will carry on without me."

In the final analysis, the gathering of Arabs, intent on annihilating the Jews in Israel while sitting at the same table with the people they wished to destroy, was contrary to all Shamir had learned from the past. He attended, however, reiterated Israel's wish for peace, did not alter his stance on anything fundamental, and returned home to Jerusalem with his overall perspective unchanged.

In mid-1993, Israeli and Palestinian representatives again engaged in peace talks, this time in Oslo, Norway. That meeting resulted in both Israel and the PLO signing the Oslo Accords, known as the Declaration of Principles, or Oslo I. The agreement was based on the 1978 Camp David Accords as signed by Israeli prime minister Menachem Begin and Egypt's Anwar Sadat. In additional Oslo documents, Israel recognized the PLO as the legitimate representative of the Palestinian people, while the PLO recognized the right of the State of Israel to exist and renounced terrorism, violence, and its desire for the destruction of Israel.

Israeli leaders and King Hussein of Jordan signed a peace agreement on October 26, 1994, in an effort to normalize relations between their two countries. The pact resolved disputes over land and water rights and opened a door for more collaboration in trade and tourism. Perhaps the most definitive clause of the treaty was the agreement that neither Israel nor Jordan would allow a third party to launch military assaults.

The Oslo II agreement was signed in 1995 and detailed the division of the West Bank into Areas A, B, and C. Area A was land under full Palestinian civilian control with the Palestinians being responsible for internal security. Area B outlined Palestinian civil control and joint Israeli–Palestinian security control. That area includes many

Oct 1994   Oct 11- 1995

Palestinian towns, villages, and areas with no Israeli settlements. Area C details full Israeli civil and security control which, by the year 2011, included 61 percent of the West Bank.

The pact further states: "Areas of the West Bank outside Areas A and B, which, except for the issues that will be negotiated in the permanent status negotiations, will be gradually transferred to Palestinian jurisdiction in accordance with this Agreement."[92] It was also during these conferences that the PLO was deliberately detached from the Palestinian people by the creation of the Palestinian Authority. Regardless, terrorism by any other name is still deadly.

16

IN THE WAKE of the signing of the Oslo Accords, President Bill Clinton formulated a comprehensive peace plan for the Middle East with Syria as the main objective. In 1994–1995, he pushed contacts between Israel and Syria into high gear; as a result, an agreement appeared to be taking shape. The proposed peace settlement, which included a complete Israeli withdrawal from the Golan Heights, awakened tremendous opposition within the Israeli populace.

Why, in spite of intelligence reports showing a likely outbreak of aggression against Israel, did the Clinton administration continue to put pressure on Israel, our most stable ally in the Middle East, to give up yet more land in the hope of securing a fragile agreement for peace? There are two important reasons why presidents Carter and Clinton and, later, President George W. Bush played the appeasement card. The first reason is that peace-agreement signings play well to the home audience. The American public has lost patience with protracted negotiations and endless rounds of international shuttle diplomacy. Most do not understand the convoluted politics of the Middle East and fail to realize that it will take far more than signatures on a series of agreements such as the Hebron Agreement, the Oslo Accords, the Road Map Plan, and the Annapolis Summit to bring true, lasting peace to the Middle East.

It was during the early days of President Clinton's administration that the United States was rocked by a devastating attack planned by Osama bin Laden's organization: the February 26, 1993, truck bombing of the World Trade Center. While this first attack was relatively ignored and quickly forgotten by many, in it were seeds of the eventual September 11, 2001, attacks at the same location. Because Mr. Clinton was more occupied with implementing his economic program than keeping America safe, his administration paid scant attention to that early event. In his regular radio address the day after the bombing, President Clinton mentioned the "tragedy" (he never once used the words *bomb* or *terrorist* in the address) and never mentioned the incident in public again. Neither did he ever visit the site of the blast. The author of *Losing bin Laden*, Richard Miniter, addressed Clinton's inability to deal with bin Laden throughout his presidency:

In 1993, bin Laden was a small-time funder of militant Muslim terrorists in Sudan, Yemen, and Afghanistan. By the end of 2000, Clinton's last year in office, bin Laden's network was operating in more than fifty-five countries and already responsible for the deaths of thousands (including fifty-five Americans).

Clinton was tested by historic, global conflict, the first phase of America's war on terror. He was president when bin Laden declared war on America. He had many chances to defeat bin Laden; he simply did not take them. If, in the wake of the 1998 embassy bombings, Clinton had rallied the public and the Congress to fight bin Laden and smash terrorism, he might have been the Winston Churchill of his generation. But, instead, he chose the role of Neville Chamberlain (whose appeasements of Hitler in Munich in 1938 are credited with paving the way to the Nazi invasion of Poland that began World War II the next year).[93]

In September of that same year, Clinton held a celebration on the White House lawn for what he called "a brave gamble for peace," where he forced—actually standing with his thumb pressed into the prime minister's back—Israel's Yitzhak Rabin to shake hands with PLO chairman Yasser Arafat,over a blank sheet of paper that represented the Declaration of Principles, or Oslo Accords. The paper lay on the same table over which President Jimmy Carter had presided, as Menachem Begin and Anwar Sadat signed the earlier peace treaty between Israel and Egypt in 1979. President Clinton later described it as one of "the highest moments" of his presidency as the two "shook hands for the first time in front of a billion people on television, it was an unbelievable day."[94]

One of Clinton's greatest hopes was to go down in history as the man who finally resolved the Arab–Israeli conflict in the Middle East. In order to do this, he used his tremendous aptitude at image transformation to turn the terrorist and murderer Yasser Arafat into a diplomat. Arafat became the most-welcomed foreign leader to the White House during the Clinton years. It also seems likely that Arafat received some coaching from Clinton and his advisors on what to say, how to speak, and what to do to help in this metamorphosis.

The late Jewish actor and spokesman Theodore Bikel said of Arafat:

> Arafat turned out to be no partner for peace . . . he had never intended to be such a partner in the first place. Oslo and the handshake gave him the cachet of peacemaker; it also gave him half of a Nobel Peace Prize, which, if he had had any sense of shame, he would have returned. In truth, for him Oslo was nothing more than an opportunity to obfuscate and spin wheels. In all the summit meetings, he appeared to be pacific, conciliatory,

and seemingly accommodating, yet he withdrew as soon as real concessions were required. . . . He never meant for the Oslo Agreement to be implemented. [95]

Reportedly, Israel's prime minister Yitzhak Rabin gave President Clinton what became known as the "deposit," a paper stating that if all of Israel's security needs were addressed and its demands regarding normalization and a withdrawal timetable were met, Israel would be willing to carry out a full retreat from the Golan Heights. The paper was only to serve to inform the president as to what Israel would be willing to do in order to ultimately attain a peace agreement. The paper was made public, and apparently Clinton betrayed Rabin, pinning the failure to reach a peace agreement on the prime minister. Seen as a traitor, Rabin was assassinated on November 5, 1995, by Yigal Amir, an Israeli extremist. What Clinton had called his "brave gamble for peace" failed miserably and certainly did not pay off for Rabin due to Clinton's interference.

In a private conversation, Prime Minister Rabin had shared with me his hopes for the restoration of his people, an end to hostilities, and the beginning of peace in the land. He told me he dreamed of his grandchildren never having to go through what he and his generation had experienced. He was a great general and a fine prime minister but keenly aware of the enormous economic pressure on his nation—and perhaps a little too willing to compromise because of it. He loved

Jerusalem and was willing to give his life for her if it came to that. Sadly, in the end, he did.

Hundreds of thousands of Israelis and visitors from abroad slowly filed past Rabin's coffin as he lay in state in the forecourt of the Knesset. In the Square in Tel Aviv where the prime minister was robbed of his life, people gathered to sing "Song for Peace":

> Let the sun rise
> Let the morning shine
> The purest prayers
> Will not bring us back
>
> He whose candle has been snuffed out
> And was buried in the ground
> Bitter tears will not wake him up
> Will not bring him back
>
> No one will resurrect us
> From the depths of darkness
> Neither the victory cheer
> Nor songs of praise will help
>
> So, sing a song for peace
> Don't whisper a prayer
> Better to cry out loud
> A song for peace.[96]

A copy of the song, soaked with Rabin's blood, had been removed from a pocket of his jacket by the hospital staff as the prime minister's life ebbed from his bullet-riddled body. World leaders and heads of state from eighty countries flew into Tel Aviv to attend Rabin's funeral—including King Hussein of Jordan, President Hosni Mubarak from Egypt, representatives from Qatar and Oman, and the prime minister of Morocco. His successor as prime minister was Shimon Peres, who said of Rabin:

> I see our people in profound shock, with tears in their eyes, but also a people who know that the bullets that murdered you could not murder the idea which you embraced. You did not leave us a last will, but you left us a path on which we will march with conviction and faith. The nation is shedding tears, but these are also tears of unity and spiritual uplifting. . . . [Then Peres quoted from Jeremiah 31:16–17] "Refrain thy voice from weeping and thine eyes from tears; for thy work shall be rewarded and there is hope for thy future, saith the Lord."[97]

Weeks later, on November 27, Peres wrote in response to sympathy letters, "His life was cut short, but not his work."[98] Peres shouldered the task of trying to continue the peace process, but his efforts were struck another blow by a series of suicide bombings. One such attack was launched on February 25 of the following year when a man boarded a bus in Jerusalem and took the lives of twenty-five people, the majority of whom were IDF soldiers. The jihadists struck Israeli civilians repeatedly, not giving a thought that Palestinians or other Arabs might be nearby. The mood in Israel tended toward despair as, one after another, suicide bombers killed and maimed people across the nation. Instead of a continuation of the peace process, Israel received only bloody acts of murder and mayhem.

The use of "smoke-and-mirror" tactics blamed a visit by the then prime minister Ariel Sharon to the Temple Mount for the launch of the Second Intifada—also called the Al-Aqsa Intifada. This move forced Israeli leaders to rethink the relationship and policies toward the Palestinians. Following a series of suicide bombings and attacks, the Israeli army launched Operation Defensive Shield. It was the largest military action conducted by Israel since the end of the Six-Day War.

As violence between the Israeli army and Palestinian militants intensified, Israel expanded its security apparatus around the West Bank by retaking many parts of land in the Area A—as had been defined in the Oslo Accords. The nation established a complicated system of roadblocks and checkpoints around major Palestinian areas to deter violence and protect Israeli settlements. However, in 2008, the IDF began to slowly transfer authority to Palestinian security forces.

Israeli prime minister Ariel Sharon instituted a policy of unilateral withdrawal from the Gaza Strip in 2003. This move was fully implemented in August 2005. Sharon's announcement to disengage from Gaza came as a tremendous shock to his critics both on the left and on the right. A year previously, he had commented that the fate of the most far-flung settlements in Gaza, Netzararem and Kfar Darom, was regarded in the same light as that of Tel Aviv.

Formal announcements to evacuate seventeen Gaza settlements and another four in the West Bank in February 2004 represented the first reversal for the settler movement since 1968. It divided Sharon's party. The move was strongly supported by Trade and Industry Minister Ehud Olmert and Tzipi Livni, the Minister for Immigration and Absorption, but Foreign Minister Silvan Shalom and Finance Minister Benjamin Netanyahu strongly condemned it. It was also uncertain whether this was simply the beginning of further evacuations.

In June 2006, Hamas militants infiltrated an army post near the Israeli side of the Gaza Strip and abducted soldier Gilad Shalit. Two IDF soldiers were killed in the attack, while Shalit was wounded as his tank was hit by a rocket. Three days later Israel launched Operation Summer Rains to secure Shalit's release. In October 18, 2011, Gilad was exchanged for 1,027 Palestinian prisoners. It speaks of the value the Israelis place on the life of just one of their own.

In July 2006, Hezbollah fighters crossed the border from Lebanon into Israel, attacking and killing eight Israeli soldiers, and abducting two others as hostages, setting off the 2006 Lebanon War, which caused widespread destruction in that country. A UN-sponsored cease-fire went into effect on August 14, 2006, officially ending the conflict.

Over a thousand Lebanese and over 150 Israelis were killed, the Lebanese civil infrastructure was severely damaged, and approximately one million Lebanese and 300,000–500,000 Israelis were displaced, although most were later able to return to their homes. After the cease-fire, some parts of southern Lebanon remained uninhabitable due to unexploded Israeli cluster bomblets.

In the aftermath of the Battle of Gaza, where Hamas seized control of the Gaza Strip in a violent civil war with rival Fatah, Israel placed restrictions on its border with Gaza and ended economic cooperation with the Palestinian leadership based there. Israel and Egypt have observed a blockade on the Gaza Strip since 2007. Israel maintains the blockade is necessary to limit Palestinian rocket attacks from Gaza and to prevent Hamas from smuggling advanced rockets and weapons capable of hitting Israeli cities.

17

ON SEPTEMBER 6, 2007, during Operation Orchard, Israel bombed an eastern Syrian complex that was reportedly a nuclear reactor being built with the assistance of North Korea. The planned attack had begun months before in a quiet Vienna neighborhood. In an article for the *New Yorker,* David Makovsky painted a graphic picture of the secret operation:

> In the first days of March, 2007, agents from the Mossad, the Israeli intelligence agency, made a daring raid on the Vienna home of Ibrahim Othman, the head of the Syrian Atomic Energy Commission. Othman was in town attending a meeting of the International Atomic Energy Agency's board of governors, and had stepped out. In less than an hour, the Mossad operatives swept in, extracted top-secret information from Othman's computer, and left without a trace. [99]

Innovative measures aren't always heralded on the front page of the *New York Times* or the *International Herald Tribune*. Such was the case when the Israeli Air Force struck a suspected nuclear site northwest of Damascus on September 6, 2007. In the aftermath of the attack, global attention focused on Syria's nuclear ambitions, but little was released about the actual incursion.

As information began to emerge, it was revealed that the attack was likely the first incidence of "electronic" combat—also called "non-kinetic" warfare.[100] The plan in such a move is to use electromagnetic transmissions to alter, destroy, or seize the opposition's military systems without initiating perceptible loss. It is, in essence, military computer hacking and electronic intelligence methods designed to reduce enemy capabilities. Israel discovered it was not only conceivable but doable.

As the incursion was being made ready, an Israeli strike force slipped into Tal Abyad, Syria, a border town near Turkey. The group disabled two radar systems, enabling Israeli jets to overfly air space without detection by the Syrian Air Force. That was a major coup, as Syrian radar defenses were considered the most complex and exhaustive in the Middle East.

The actual bombing run was carried out by ten Israeli F-15I *Ra'am* fighter jets attached to the Israeli Air Force 69th Squadron. The aircraft were armed with "laser-guided bombs, escorted by F-16I *Sufa* fighter jets and a few [electronic intelligence]. . . aircraft....Three of the

F-15s were ordered back to base, while the remaining seven continued towards Syria."[101]

Following the attack, Israeli prime minister Ehud Olmert contacted Turkish prime minister Recep Tayyip Erdoğan to inform him of the circumstances. Erdoğan was then asked to forward a communiqué to Syria's Assad. The message in blunt form: "Don't try to build another nuclear plant." The Syrian dictator was urged not to make media fodder of the attack and was assured the Israelis would show restraint as well.

CNN was the first to report the bombing; Olmert's comment was:

> The security services and Israeli defense forces are demonstrating unusual courage. We naturally cannot always show the public our cards.[102]

Questions to Israeli sources regarding how the feat was accomplished were met with restrained silence. According to Makovsky:

> The next day, the Syrian Arab News Agency announced that Israeli planes had entered Syrian airspace but had been repelled: "Air-defense units confronted them and forced them to leave after they dropped some ammunition in deserted areas without causing any human or material damage." The Israelis say that not a single Syrian air-defense missile was launched. At least

ten, and perhaps as many as three dozen, workers were killed in the strike.[103]

In April 2008, Syrian president Bashar al-Assad told a Qatari newspaper that Syria and Israel had been discussing a peace treaty for a year, with Turkey as a go-between. This was confirmed in May of that year by a spokesman for Prime Minister Olmert. As well as a peace treaty, the future of the Golan Heights was discussed. President Assad vowed negotiations with Israel would be forestalled until a new US president took office.

Earlier, in 1988 a new entity arose in the Middle East: *Harakut al-Muqawama al-Islamiyya* (Islamic Resistance). Founded by Sheikh Ahmed Yassin, this offshoot of the Muslim Brotherhood would become known by the Hebrew acronym *Hamas*. In August of that year, it would make public its covenant. Among the articles published is this declaration:

> The day that enemies usurp part of Moslem land, Jihad becomes the individual duty of every Moslem. In face of the Jews' usurpation of Palestine, it is compulsory that the banner of Jihad be raised. To do this requires the diffusion of Islamic consciousness among the masses, both on the regional, Arab and Islamic levels. It is necessary to instill the spirit of Jihad in the heart of the nation

so that they would confront the enemies and join the ranks of the fighters.[104]

Dedicated to maiming and murdering Jews, Hamas would join the ranks of other terrorist organizations. This faction has both social and religious arms, operating medical facilities and madrassas (schools). Funds raised for these two subsidiaries are funneled to the military branch. The indoctrination of young Palestinians is a useful means to recruit anti-Semitic suicide bombers determined to attack targets in Israel.

Targets in Israel beginning in the mid-1990s have included buses, malls, restaurants, and hotels. Examples of murder and mayhem include the Sbarro Pizza attack in Jerusalem that resulted in fifteen dead and 130 injured. Another even more deadly attack targeted a Passover Seder at the Park Hotel in Netanya. Thirty were killed and 140 injured. Once Israel's leaders were pressured by world opinion to relinquish the Gaza Strip to Hamas, it became the launching pad for thousands of rocket launches into Israel. The cities of Sderot, Ashkelon, and Netivot in the south were targets. In more recent years, Hamas rockets have reached Tel Aviv, Jerusalem, Be'er Sheva (Beersheba), and even the more northern city of Haifa.

In 2005, Hamas gained enough seats in the Palestinian Authority to become a viable entity in the governing process. Hamas leader Ismail Haniyeh was proclaimed prime minister of the PA alongside

Mahmoud Abbas, its president. Hamas was called upon to meet three conditions in order to receive financial aid from outside sources: (1) renounce terrorism; (2) recognize Israel's right to exist; and (3) concede to agreements already in place between Israel and the PA. To date, none of these conditions have been met.

The uneasy pact between Hamas and the PA ended in June 2007 when the two groups engaged in fighting in Gaza. Abbas stepped in and declared his own version of martial law and assumed emergency powers over the governing body. Attempts to reconcile the two entities, including one in 2014, have been unsuccessful.

In December 2008, Israel retaliated for the thousands of rocket attacks by launching Operation Cast Lead. It was a three-week military operation designed to halt the air assaults and end Hamas's trafficking in war materiel.

A raid was carried out by Israeli naval forces on six ships of the *Gaza Freedom Flotilla* in May 2010. The ships refused to dock at Port Ashdod. On the MV *Mavi Marmara*, activists clashed with an Israeli boarding party. During the fighting, nine activists were killed by Israeli Special Forces. Widespread international condemnation followed. Relations between Israel and Turkey were strained, and Israel subsequently eased its blockade on the Gaza Strip. Several dozen passengers and seven Israeli soldiers were injured.

Following yet another round of peace talks between Israel and the Palestinian Authority, thirteen Palestinian militant movements led by Hamas initiated a terror campaign designed to derail and disrupt the negotiations. Attacks on Israelis increased in August 2010, after four civilians were killed by Hamas terrorists.

Palestinian militants increased the frequency of rocket attacks aimed at Israelis, and on August 2, Hamas launched seven Katyusha rockets at Eilat and Aqaba, killing one Jordanian civilian and wounding four others.

Intermittent fighting has continued, including 680 rocket attacks on Israel in 2011 alone. On November 14, 2012, Israeli forces killed Ahmed Jabari, a leader of Hamas's military wing, launching Operation Pillar of Defense. Hamas and Israel agreed to an Egyptian-mediated cease-fire on November 21 of that year.

The Palestinian Centre for Human Rights claimed that 158 Palestinians had been killed during the operation, of which: 102 were civilians, 55 were militants and one was a policeman; 30 were children and 13 were women.

B'Tselem (the Israeli Information Center for Human Rights in the Occupied Territories) stated that according to its initial findings, which covered only the period in mid-November, 102 Palestinians were killed in the Gaza Strip, 40 of them civilians. According to Israeli figures, 120 combatants and 57 civilians were killed.

International outcry ensued, with many criticizing Israel for what much of the international community perceived as a disproportionately violent response. Protests took place on hundreds of college campuses across the United States and in front of the Israeli consulate in New York. Additional protests followed throughout the Middle East, Europe, and in parts of South America.

Operation Protective Edge in July 2014 was a fifty-day operation to halt the launching by Hamas of further missiles and rockets into Israel. During the skirmishes, Hamas launched 4,700 projectiles into Israel. Numerous human rights organizations accused both Israel and Hamas of committing war crimes.

The governments of the United States, the United Kingdom, and Canada have expressed support for Israel's right to defend herself, and/or condemned the ongoing Hamas rocket attacks on Israel. And so the relentless conflict between Israel and the Arab world continues, abated only occasionally by short-lived pacts, agreements, and accords that are broken with impunity by those who wish to see Israel annihilated.

18

IN 1999, a group of separatists split from al-Qaeda. It would gain prominence in June 2014 when it declared a new caliphate. It has been alternately known as ISIS—the Islamic State of Iraq and Syria; IS—Islamic State; ISIL—Islamic State of Iraq and the Levant; and *Daesh, al-Dawla al-Islamiya fi al-Iraq wa al-Sham*, and "Depending on how it is conjugated in Arabic, it can mean anything from 'to trample down and crush' to 'a bigot who imposes his view on others.'"[105] Islamic State leaders have threatened to remove the tongue of any individual using what they consider to be a pejorative term.

Since the winter of 2015, ISIS has increased its presence, power, and rule in the area near the border between Israel and Syria. The concern is that the cancer of ISIS will metastasize, feeding on global oil to nurture and ultimately change the balance of the contest in the Middle East. For Israel, it is just one more threat to her security.

In March 2015, Prime Minister Netanyahu summed up the enemies of Israel very succinctly:

2015

Iran's regime is as radical as ever. Its cries of death to America, that same America that it calls the great Satan, as loud as ever. Now, this should not be surprising because the ideology of Iran's revolutionary regime is deeply rooted in militant Islam. That is why this regime will always be an enemy of America.

Don't be fooled. The battle between Iran and ISIS doesn't turn Iran into a friend of America. Iran and ISIS are competing for the crown of militant Islam. One calls itself the Islamic Republic and the other calls itself the Islamic State. Both want to impose a militant Islamic empire, first on the region and then on the entire world.

They just disagree among themselves who will be the ruler of that empire. In this deadly game of thrones, there is no place for America or for Israel, no peace for Christians, Jews, or Muslims who don't share the Islamist medieval creed. No rights for women. No freedom for anyone. So when it comes to Iran and ISIS, the enemy of your enemy is your enemy.[106]

Netanyahu's warnings seemingly fell on deaf ears when in July of 2015 Secretary of State John Kerry, with the approval of President Barack Obama, signed a deal with the Iranians that opened wide the door for Iran to regain its superpower status in the Middle East.

President Obama was jubilant in yet another effort to establish a legacy for his presidency that places the entire world at risk. In remarks that were broadcast in Iran, he boasted, "This deal offers an opportunity to move in a new direction. We should seize it."[107]

By autumn 2016, a new genre of intifada had found its way to the streets of Jerusalem. The new flood of Palestinian terrorism took the form of so-called "lone wolf" attacks by knife, automobile, or attempted kidnappings. In that year, ninety Israelis died in 122 terror attacks with 381 wounded. In July 2017, yet another attempt was made by a Palestinian to ram a group with a vehicle. When that failed, he jumped from the car and charged the bystanders with a knife. IDF soldiers shot the attacker in what seemingly has become another day in the life of a nation endangered by anti-Semitism.

In mid-July of that same year, another young Israeli paid the ultimate sacrifice. Like most young people of her generation, Hadas Malka was adept at using social media. So on a Friday evening she sent a selfie taken by the wall of Jerusalem to friends and family that read, "Shabbat Shalom to my loving friends." Fifteen minutes later, 23-year-old Hadas was dead. A member of Israel's Border Guard Police, she was stabbed to death by a Palestinian terrorist in an attack near the historic Damascus Gate leading into the Old City of Jerusalem. She had volunteered for the more hazardous duty with the Border Guard Police because she was willing to put her life on the line to defend her country. She paid the ultimate price that so many before her have paid. And her death is a grim reminder of the nature of the threats facing the Jewish people in today's world.

Still another attack took place on July 14, 2017. Three terrorists opened fire on a group of policemen near Jerusalem's Lions' Gate. Two of the officers were killed and two wounded. The weapons used in the attack had been taken onto the Temple Mount by an accomplice and hidden in Al-Aqsa Mosque.

The terrorists then made their way into the Old City and to the mosque to retrieve the backpack with the guns stashed inside. After the attack, the men fled back onto the Temple Mount. Israeli police opened fire on the terrorists, killing them on the esplanade of the complex. Prior to the assault, one of the gunmen, Mohammad Hamed Jabreen, posted a selfie of himself standing in front of the Dome of the Rock. He included the message: "Tomorrow's smile will be more beautiful, God willing."

Both for security reasons and to search for additional hidden weapons, the Old City and the Temple Mount were immediately closed to traffic and remained shuttered on Saturday, July 15. The closure was the first time in nearly fifty years that access had been forbidden on the Islamic holy day. On Sunday, July 16, the Temple Mount was reopened but with the addition of cameras and metal detectors to prevent the smuggling of weapons onto the mount. The closure resulted in demonstrations against Israel in adjoining Arab countries.

The deal with the Iranians has done little, if anything, to discourage terrorism in Israel. How could it when the ayatollahs, imams, and mullahs in that Shi'ite country regularly call for the annihilation of Israel, to see its inhabitants "wiped from the face of the earth"? Prime Minister Netanyahu called the deal "a jackpot, a cash bonanza of hundreds of billions of dollars, which will enable it to continue to pursue its aggression and terror in the region and in the world."[108] It also ended the European oil embargo and flooded an already oil-glutted economy with even more oil. Financial restraints on Iranian banks also ceased with the inking of the deal.

Israel and members of the US House and Senate were not the only ones who opposed the lessening of restrictions on Iran; Sunni Arab nations were highly skeptical of any plan that would leave Iran with the ability to produce the materials necessary for the production of atomic weapons. In a decade, the deal would expire, leaving Iran with the existing substructure necessary to produce an atomic bomb. Add to that the report that the "binding agreement" pushed by the Obama administration was never even signed by the Iranians. In an article by *National Review* journalist Joel Gehrke, the State Department assistant secretary for legislative affairs, Julia Frifield, wrote to Representative Mike Pompeo of Kansas. In her missive, Frifield stated,

> The Joint Comprehensive Plan of Action (JCPOA)
> is not a treaty or an executive agreement, and is not

a signed document . . . [She continued] The success
of the JCPOA will depend not on whether it is legally
binding or signed, but rather on the extensive verifica-
tion measures we have put in place, as well as Iran's
understanding that we have the capacity to re-impose—
and ramp up—our sanctions if Iran does not meet its
commitments.[109]

The document contained provisions for a five-year extension
of the UN arms embargo, but that, too, could be suspended if the
Iranians can pass IAEA inspections. A UN curb on the transfer-
ence of technology relating to ballistic missiles to Iran could stay
in place for an additional eight years. Of course, Russia and China
cried foul because of the presence of ISIL in the region. As might
be expected, the Iranians also rejected a noteworthy part of the
treaty that would permit inspections of military sites. Iran's Supreme
Leader Ayatollah Ali Khamenei was, and still is, adamantly opposed
to such intrusion. Therefore, access is not assured. It appears
that the deal was skewed in Iran's favor before the ink had even
dried.

According to the pact, the US Congress was given a sixty-day
period in which to review the deal, an evaluation that might have
gone against President Obama. He would, however, still have had veto
power. The president's plan was little more than a *quid pro quo*—a

get-out-of-jail card for an appeasement plan that would allow Iran's leaders to creep out from under the harsh sanctions that had brought them to the table in the first place.

Jerusalem Post writer Michael Wilner explained what might happen in Iran's end game:

> But the concerns of Prime Minister Benjamin Netanyahu . . . when he publicly fought the agreement, were twofold. He firstly worried that Iran would violate the deal in undetectable ways—through undeclared channels and facilities, too sophisticated for the inspections regime to pick up on. But he secondly feared that Iran would abide by the agreement to a tee; that the agreement would allow Iran to glide toward an internationally legitimatized, industrial-sized nuclear program once several of these sunset provisions expire. And the political ramifications of this second concern will not reverberate for several more years.[110]

In 2007, I wrote *The Final Move Beyond Iraq: The Final Solution While the World Sleeps*. In that book is the following statement:

> Appeasement has been the offshoot of self-loathing. We hate war rather than believe that those who wage war against us are evil. The liberal left believes we are evil

by retaliating, or even worse by striking preemptively to prevent danger. Self-loathing replaces righteous indignation and begets appeasement. The desire to negotiate no matter the cost gives rise to those of the West who unwittingly become cohorts to the jihadists. These individuals rationalize the presence of evil and attacks by terrorists based on their perception of our own past sins.

19

WHEN THE STATE OF ISRAEL was reborn in 1948, there were slightly more than one million Jews in Palestine. Today that number has grown to over six million. Despite terror attacks, loss of life, and wavering world opinion, Israeli society has become more interconnected. Critics consider it to have been a necessity in the first years of the reborn state but now assert that there is no longer a need for it. Others, mainly Mizrahi Jews (descended from local communities of the Middle East, as opposed to those from Europe), along with Holocaust survivors, have criticized the earlier move to unify the country. According to them, they were forced to conceal their diaspora heritage and philosophies brought from other countries, and adopt a new Sabra culture. The word *Sabra* originally described the new Jew that had emerged in Palestine, particularly when contrasted with the old Jew from overseas.

Israel's culture—literature, arts, music, dance, theater, and media—is fertile, alive, and energetic. It is comprised of a plethora of inspiration, from the rich culture of czarist Russia, to the halls of academia, from the influences of craftsmen, bankers, writers, and artists, to the busy streets housing jewelers in Amsterdam. It grew stronger through the struggles of wars, pogroms, and the staggering anti-Semitism that seemed to plague Jews in every country where they settled. As the suffering in the life of the hunted and haunted drifts through the pages of Jewish literature, it both stirs the senses and raises awareness. For example:

✦ *Death of a Salesman* (1949) by Arthur Miller
Miller's play tells the tale of Willy Loman, but also works as the perfect parable of the death of the American Dream.

✦ *The Catcher in the Rye* (1951) by J. D. Salinger
No list dealing with best fiction of the last century would be complete without Salinger's ode to teenage angst, and the limited knowledge we have of the late writer tells us that this book was indeed the product of Jewish neurosis.

✦ *Maus: A Survivor's Tale* (1986) by Art Spiegelman
The only comic book to ever win the Pulitzer Prize. Art Spiegelman's biography of his father's life before, during and after the Holocaust, brought the medium to a whole new level.

✧ *The Pawnbroker* by Edward Lewis Wallant

The story of a holocaust survivor attempting to live with his demons will haunt you long after you've read it.

✧ *Comedy in a Minor Key* (2010) by Hans Keilson

It took about 100 years, but Hans Keilson was finally recognized as one of the world's greatest writers. This book about a young Dutch couple that takes in a sick Jewish man during World War 2—only to find themselves trying to figure out how to cover up his death—isn't the sort of dark comedy that leaves you chuckling. It's the sort that makes you exclaim, "that's brilliant."[111]

While Hebrew and Arabic are the official languages of the State, an incredible eighty-three tongues are spoken in the country. As new immigrants began to arrive, learning Hebrew became a national goal. Special schools for the teaching of Hebrew were set up all over the country.

The initial works of Hebrew literature in Israel were written by authors rooted in the world and traditions of European Jewry. Native-born writers who published their works in the 1940s and 1950s, often called the "War of Independence generation," brought the Sabra mentality and culture to their writing.

Israeli culture is neither static nor one-dimensional; it is growing, evolving, and illuminating the complex nature of the very culture it reflects. So many immigrants contribute to the wealth of the society, it would be impossible to attribute its richness and ideology to any one group.

The Jewish infusion from other countries, for instance, brought classical music to the fore in Israel. It has been especially vibrant as hundreds of music teachers and students, composers, instrumentalists and singers, as well as thousands of music lovers streamed into the country, driven initially by the threat of Nazism in Europe. Israel is home to several world-class classical music ensembles, such as the Israel Philharmonic and the New Israeli Opera.

The founding of the Palestine Philharmonic Orchestra (today's Israel Philharmonic Orchestra) in 1936 marked the beginning of Israel's classical music scene. In the early 1980s, the New Israeli Opera began staging productions, reviving public enthusiasm for operatic works. Russian immigration in the 1990s boosted the classical music genre with new talents and music lovers. The Israel Philharmonic Orchestra performs at venues throughout the country and abroad, and almost every city has its own orchestra, many of the musicians having emigrated from the former Soviet Union.

Popular music was influenced in the 1960s by French entertainers, but in more recent decades, that honor has gone to the United States, Great Britain, Europe, and as far afield as South America. The twenty-first century has brought musicians from Turkish, Greek, and Arab cultures to the forefront.

Israeli filmmakers and thespians have been given accolades and awards at international film festivals. At one time, the only Israeli imports in Hollywood were producers. The most well-known actor was Topol, who received acclaim in *Fiddler on the Roof*. In recent years, however, Israeli actors have graduated from bit parts and roles as villains to starring roles in major motion pictures. One young woman, Gal Gadot, a former Miss Israel (2004) and once an IDF soldier, won acclaim in the 2017 blockbuster movie *Wonder Woman*.

The Israeli film industry has branched out to include films that showcase an individual and his or her personal sufferings and challenges, as well as films that tell stories as they relate to social and political struggles. Many of the films have garnered worldwide commendation.

In recent decades, Jewish literature has been widely translated, and several Israeli writers have gained international recognition. Among those men and women who have excelled and won praise are writers Martin Buber, Anne Frank, Amos Oz, Elie Wiesel, and Leah Goldberg. Historians and politicians who gained commendation are Abba Eban, Yitzhak Rabin, his wife, Leah Rabin, Menachem Begin, Golda Meir, Benjamin Netanyahu, and Chaim Herzog. Among contemporary authors to watch are Dalia Betolin-Sherman, who immigrated to Israel from Ethiopia and is the first woman to publish a volume in Hebrew, along with Merav Nakar Sadi, who was awarded the Sapir Prize—a prestigious annual literary award for works in Hebrew—for the best debut novel. Also on the list are Dror Burstein, who is also a full-time professor at Tel Aviv University, and Sapir Prize nominee, mystery writer Dror Mishani.

From the beginning of the twentieth century, visual arts in Israel have shown a creative orientation, influenced both by the West and East, as well as by the land itself. Their developments, the character of the cities, and stylistic trends have been imported from art centers abroad. In painting, sculpture, photography, and other art forms, the country's varied landscape is prominent: the hill terraces and ridges produce special dynamics of line and shape; the foothills of the Negev, the prevailing grayish-green vegetation, and the clear luminous light result in distinctive color effects; and the sea and sand affect surfaces. Local landscapes, concerns, and politics ensure the uniqueness of Israeli art.

Traditional folk music of Israel includes the Hora and Yemenite dances. Modern dance in Israel has gained international acclaim. Israeli choreographers are considered to be among the most versatile and original international creators working today. Notable dance companies include the Batsheva Dance Company and the Kibbutz Contemporary Dance Company. People come from all over Israel and many other nations for the annual dance festival staged each July in Karmiel. It is the largest celebration of dance in Israel, featuring three or four days and nights of dancing, with 5,000 or more dancers and a quarter of a million spectators visiting the capital of Galilee. Begun as an Israeli folk dance event, festivities now include performances, workshops, and open dance sessions featuring a variety of dance forms and nationalities. Famous companies and choreographers from all over the world have come to Israel to perform and give master classes.

Israel has the highest number of museums per capita in the world, with over two hundred attracting millions of visitors annually. Jerusalem's Israel Museum has a special pavilion showcasing the Dead Sea Scrolls and a large collection of Jewish religious art, Israeli art, sculptures, and Old Masters paintings. Yad Vashem, the nation of Israel's memorial to Holocaust victims, is one of the most-visited sites in the country. The holy halls preserve and cherish memories of those who perished in ovens fired by hatred, and disclose the lessons learned for future generations.

In September 2015, the Friends of Zion Heritage Center and Museum at 20 Rivlin Street in Jerusalem was officially opened and dedicated. It has long been a dream of this author to make it possible for the Jewish people and the world to know the love that millions have for God's chosen people. What a milestone for this vision and the future of Israel to see its doors opened! Through this marvelous museum, we tell the stories of heroes of the faith who sacrificed everything—including some of whom sacrificed their very lives—to protect the Jewish people.

20

ISRAEL'S DIVERSE culture is manifested in its cuisine, a combination of local ingredients and dishes and diasporic dishes from around the world. An Israeli "fusion" cuisine has developed, with the adoption and continued adaptation of elements of various Jewish dishes along with other foods traditionally eaten in the Middle East. Israeli cuisine is understandably influenced in great measure by geography, featuring foods common in the Mediterranean region such as olives, chickpeas, dairy products, fish, and fresh fruits and vegetables.

Israel's main meal is usually lunch rather than dinner. Additionally, Jewish holidays influence the fare, with many traditional foods served. Shabbat (the Jewish day of rest and seventh day of the week) dinner, eaten on Friday night, is a significant meal in many Israeli homes. While not all Jews in Israel keep kosher, the observance of *kashrut*, or Israeli dietary laws, influences the menu in numerous homes, public institutions, and many restaurants. Food that may be consumed according to Jewish law is termed "kosher" in English, or fit for consumption. Most of the basic laws of kashrut are derived from the Torah's Books of Leviticus and Deuteronomy. While the Torah does not state the rationale for most kashrut laws, many reasons have been suggested, chief among them philosophical, practical, and hygienic.

Since physical fitness is important in Jewish culture, the Maccabiah Games, an Olympic-style event for Jewish athletes, was first held in 1932 in British Mandate Palestine. The games were suspended between 1938 and 1950; when they resumed, it was in the independent State of Israel. The games have been held in Israel every four years since then in the year following the Summer Olympics.

At this writing, Israelis have won nine Olympic medals dating from their initial victories in 1992, including a gold medal in windsurfing at the 2004 Summer Olympics, and two medals in judo at the 2016 games in Rio de Janeiro, Brazil. Although the Olympic Games should showcase cooperation and brotherhood, sadly, it has not been true for the Israelis. The events in Munich in 1972 should have been horrific enough to encourage inclusion from that time forward, but anti-Semitism still dominates some of the participating nations. In 2016's judo competition, a Saudi Arabian female competitor, Joud Fahmy, forfeited her competition against Gili Cohen rather than compete against an Israeli. In the male competition, Egyptian Islam El Shehaby lost his first-round match to Or Sasson of Israel. When Sasson reached out to shake the hand of his opponent at the end of the match, the Egyptian declined. Apparently the peace treaty in existence between the two countries does not extend to the Olympics.

Jealousy could likely be the reason fundamental Islamists fanatically target not only the Jews in Israel but also United States citizens, according to noted Jewish lecturer Irwin N. Graulich:

> The double standard with regard to Israel runs quite deeply. Indeed, no rational rules apply. Throughout history, after a victory in war, the victor determines the terms of peace. However, when Israel is victorious in three consecutive wars [1948, 1967, 1973], it must beg for peace and recognition of existence. For Israel, winning the battle only means the right to return everything and be nice to the enemy. . . .
>
> In addition, during that same period [1948–current], Israel totally embarrassed the entire Arab/Muslim world by defeating them economically, technologically, intellectually, culturally, religiously, medically, socially and morally. Since America's accomplishments are that much greater, it is no wonder that the Arab/Muslim nations feel totally frustrated. They subscribe to a religious belief that promises world greatness, strength and domination, while reality shows them trailing very far behind.[112]

Not only are there numerous inventive and creative people in Israel, there is also a sense of generosity and compassion few of its neighbors deign to recognize and/or accept. For example, a 2002 *World News* article revealed a heartwarming story of unheralded assistance to a family in Syria:

> The young girl was dying when she arrived in the land of her country's enemy. A heart condition had left the 4-year-old Syrian struggling to walk or even talk. But in Israel—a country still in a state of cease-fire with Syria after the Yom Kippur War four decades ago—she found her saviors. Admitted [in early 2013] to the Wolfson Medical Center, south of Tel Aviv, she underwent life-saving surgery. The girl is now recuperating on a ward along with children from the West Bank and Gaza Strip, Sudan, Romania, China and Israel. "She would have definitely died if she wouldn't have arrived here," Ilan Cohen, one of the doctors who treated her, said. "A lot of patients arrive here from enemy countries and view Israelis as demons. They are surprised that we are human without horns on our heads," he added. "This is the first time they see Israelis without a uniform and I think it's a good surprise." Her treatment was the work of "Save a Child's Heart," an Israeli nonprofit organization started

by the late Ami Cohen, who moved to Israel from the United States in 1992. He joined the staff of the Wolfson with a vision to mending children's hearts from around the world. The organization he began has since helped treat 3,200 children from 45 countries.[113]

The story told of the mother's fear of reprisal upon the family's return home. It seems incredible that hatred could be so strong as to fault a family for trying to save a beloved child; and yet it is. The other side of that story is the men and women who provided the techniques and services that saved the life of the young girl.

In the sixty-five-plus years since Israel was recognized as a state in the mid-1940s, amazing strides have been made in science, technology, medicine, farming, and communication thanks to the diligence of the people who live in the Holy Land.

There have been some mind-boggling discoveries in the field of medicine:

✧ In 1954, Ephraim Frei discovered the effects of magnetism on the human body. His exploration led to the advancement of the T-Scan system, a breakthrough in the advancement for detecting breast cancer.

✧ In 1956, Professor Leo Sachs developed amniocentesis to uncover the benefits of examining amniotic fluid in the diagnosis of prenatal anomalies. It has become a major obstetrics tool in aiding pregnant women and their unborn babies. In 1963, Sachs became the first to grow lab-bred blood cells, a tool used to help chemotherapy patients.

✧ Ada Yonath, awarded the Nobel Prize in Chemistry in 2009, laid the groundwork for the advent of drugs that are used to treat some strains of leukemia, glaucoma, and HIV, as well as antipsychotic and antidepressant medicines.

✧ The time it takes to heal a broken bone may soon be cut in half thanks to an intelligent "wrapping paper" from Israeli company Regenecure. The "wrapping paper," technically called a membrane implant, enables bones to heal faster and more evenly by attracting healing stem cells and fluids while keeping soft tissues from growing around the broken bone. The membrane looks and feels like plastic wrap, it can be cut with a pair of scissors to fit any bone in the body and is naturally absorbed into the body after 10 months. The material has already been used in dental procedures to replace bone grafts and has been used on animal bones, where it cut the healing time in half when used along with a traditional bone graft.[114]

Added to these inspired and ingenious men and women are Meir Wilchek, the discoverer of blood detoxification; Elli Canaani, inventing a drug to treat chronic myelogenous leukemia; Avram Hershko and Aaron Ciechanover, improving cellular research to better determine the cause of ailments such as cervical cancer and cystic fibrosis; and the creation of Copaxone, the only non-interferon treatment for multiple sclerosis. These are but a few of the many advancements in detection and management of a myriad of diseases and serious health conditions. Amazing and innovative techniques have originated in the field of spinal surgery, treatment of Parkinson's disease, tumor and small bowel (PillCam™) imaging, in first-aid in the form of innovative field dressings that are now the global standard, the LuboCollar, used to treat trauma patients worldwide, helping paraplegics walk, treating diabetes, artificial limb improvements, and more.

Israel has silently and steadily blossomed into an enthusiastic and impressive proving ground for entrepreneurs and inventors. In the field of technology, just a few examples are:

The Uzi machine gun developed by Major Uzi Gaf; millions are in use globally.

The WEIZAC computer introduced by the Weizmann Institute in 1955 was one of the first, "large-scale stored program computers in the world."[115]

A solar energy system that today is used to power the majority of hot water heaters worldwide. We must also include color holograms, desalination processes, drone aircraft, computer processors, digital information sharing, terrorist detectors, and thousands of other technology-based products.[116]

Farmers worldwide have enjoyed the benefits of advances such as the super cucumber and a disease-resistant potato, improved food-storage systems, drip irrigation, extracting water from the air, bee preservation, advanced fish farming, water purification, and more ecologically friendly food packaging.

Add to this list baby monitors, instant messaging, office equipment, the Babylon computer dictionary, flash drives, microcomputers, miniature video cameras, computer chips, advances in airport safety, and missile defense systems. It is an incredible list, a testament to the ingenuity and inventiveness of the Jewish people.

Many of these inventions have earned Nobel Prizes for those responsible, but the awards are not confined to science and technology. Now they are shared by Israeli authors, poets, mathematicians, peacemakers, and economists.

It is amazing to discover that 22 percent of all individual Nobel Prize winners worldwide between the organization's inception in

1901 and 2015 have been of Jewish descent. That alone is an incredible number to contemplate.

Imre Kertész and Elie Wiesel are two Jewish laureates who were honored after having endured incarceration in concentration camps during the Holocaust. At the age of fourteen, Kertész was rounded up with other Hungarian Jews and sent first to Auschwitz, then to Buchenwald. He is a prolific writer whose best-known novel, *Sorstalanság* (Fateless), unveiled the experiences of a teenage boy who was sent to the camps at Auchwitz, Buchenwald, and Zeitz. He was awarded the Prize in 2002 "for writing that upholds the fragile experience of the individual against the barbaric arbitrariness of history."[117]

Elie Wiesel, who was also sent to Auschwitz, Buna, and Buchenwald during World War II, received the Nobel Prize in 1986. The committee characterized him as a "messenger to mankind," stating that through his struggle to come to terms with "his own personal experience of total humiliation and of the utter contempt for humanity shown in Hitler's death camps," as well as his "practical work in the cause of peace," Wiesel delivered a powerful message "of peace, atonement and human dignity" to humanity.

21

IT IS INCREDIBLY overwhelming to consider how many life-changing inventions might have been lost at Auschwitz and Birkenau, only two of the many concentration camps where Jews were cruelly treated and murdered during the Holocaust.

While the slaughter was unimaginable, there are some who blindly contend that the brutality and death never occurred. There are, however, countless survivors who bear witness to the awful crimes against humanity. Among those who escaped before the noose closed around the necks of millions of Jews was the family of Professor Robert Aumann.

In 2009, I was invited to speak at a communications and law conference held at Ariel University in Israel. It was my distinct privilege to meet Nobel Laureate and founder of the Game Theory Society, Professor Aumann of Hebrew University. I had been asked to attend the conference by my good friend the late Ron Nachman, former mayor of the city of Ariel, and was able to view firsthand the genius of the professor.

Born in Germany, Aumann and his family escaped just fourteen days before the ravages of *Kristallnacht*, the beginning of a series of coordinated attacks against Jews in Nazi Germany and parts of Austria. In a 2005 *Jerusalem Post* article, journalist Hilary Leila Krieger wrote:

> The year was 1938 and the Aumanns desperately wanted to leave their native Germany. Salvation dangled in the form of US visas, available for passport holders who swore they wouldn't be a burden on their new country and passed a test of basic American terms and concepts. Robert "Yisrael" Aumann saw his parents studying hard and thought he should do likewise. After his parents passed the exam, his mother confided in the consular official that her son had also prepared very diligently and would like to be presented with a test question. The consul leaned over to the eight-year-old and asked him to name the president of the United States—at the time Franklin D. Roosevelt. Aumann answered enthusiastically: "Rosenfeld!" The consul burst out laughing. He also granted the boy a visa. The qualities Aumann displayed at a ripe age—a propensity for hard work, a fierce intellect

and a commitment to Jewish values—and has continued to exhibit throughout adulthood, earned him [the] Nobel prize in economics.[119]

When presented with the Nobel Prize in 2005, the professor titled his acceptance speech "War and Peace." He said to the assembled audience, "Simplistic peacemaking can cause war, while an arms race, credible war threats and mutually assured destruction can reliably prevent war."[120]

Noted author Ernest Hemingway wrote: "The world breaks everyone, and afterward, some are strong at the broken places."[121] Indeed, adversity has forged a people of great strength, resiliency, insight, and intelligence. As the psalmist wrote in Psalm 115:12 (ESV): "The LORD has remembered us; he will bless us; he will bless the house of Israel . . ."

The list of Nobel Prize–winning men and women who have sprung from Abraham, Isaac, and Jacob is long and impressive: Nelly Sachs, Shmuel Yosef Agnon, Saul Bellow, Ada Yonath, Isaac Bashevis Singer, the afore-mentioned Robert Aumann, Dan Shechtman, former leaders Menachem Begin, Yitzhak Rabin, and Shimon Peres.

However, brilliance, tenacity, and determination are not confined to Nobel Prize winners. It is found in all men and women whose goals are to work hard, teach their children, bless their neighbors, feed the hungry, extend a helping hand to those in need, and build on the foundations of the past to reap the blessings of Jehovah—He who blesses the House of Israel.

Twenty-first-century Jewish scientists and inventors can also be found at the forefront of creative ability and technological genius. Just as in past decades, Israelis are not simply marginal participants in new and innovative discoveries; they are at the very epicenter of modern ingenuity.

In recent years, however, the fight against Israel's very existence has taken yet another downward turn—targeting the nation's productivity. While Jewish men and women work to make the world a better place, a demonic plan has been birthed in hell to destroy the nation of Israel—to literally bankrupt her and curse the nation. It is called BDS—Boycott, Divestment, and Sanctions—and is all about economics. The plan is to turn worldwide public opinion against Israel, to isolate the Jewish nation, decimate her economy, and reshape Israel into a pariah state that no one person will be willing to defend.

Global pension funds have hastened to join this movement. The Rand Corporation reports that if this trend continues, the BDS movement would cost Israel more than $47 billion. Some of the most powerful names supporting BDS include business magnate George Soros, and even Bill Gates, co-founder of Microsoft. Universities around the world are also behind the movement and count among their number some of America's leading schools.

A number of performing artists have joined the boycott against Israel, including, Bono, Snoop Dogg, Bjork, Mia Farrow, Madonna, Jean-Luc Godard, Elvis Costello, Gil Scott-Heron, Carlos Santana, and others.[122] And the Jewish nation is also being blacklisted. For example, both the Luxembourg and Norway Pension Funds have nixed any involvement with Israel.

Regardless, the tenth and current president of Israel, Reuven Rivlin, has said that his nation is accustomed to debate and denunciation. In an opinion editorial for *Ynetnews* in 2016, Rivlin wrote:

> I'm sorry to say that some parts of BDS even include factions which are connected to enemies of the State of Israel, and who work in order to eradicate Israel as a Jewish state. Some of them are even worse, and hide their anti-Semitism by calling their actions "criticism of Israeli policy." . . . The BDS movement, as a movement which rejects Israel's existence, has on multiple occasions spread modern-day blood libels. It doesn't advance peace, but hatred. It is our responsibility to take apart this organization. . . . Boycotts, violence, and incitement only deepen divides, and don't bring us any closer to a solution. When BDS takes over, criticism turns into camouflage for the de-legitimization of the existence of the State of Israel.[123]

Perhaps the last person one might assume would deny the validity of the BDS movement would be a pro-Palestinian such as Norman Finkelstein. This political scientist averred that this particular organization could be deemed a cult controlled by the Palestinian Authority. Finkelstein charged BDS supporters with misrepresenting what was deemed to be Israel's obligation under laws established by the International Court of Justice, itself a weak, namby-pamby, and "incapable of rendering impartial justice."[124]

As of this writing, the BDS movement seems to be losing steam, but there are other groups waiting to rush in, castigate Israel, and fill the vacuum left by that organization.

Perhaps the most heartbreaking thing about this demonic conspiracy is the number of church organizations that have been practicing divestment. The Presbyterian Church of the USA is part of this movement, as are the United Church of Christ, the United Methodist Church, the Quaker Friends Fiduciary Corporation, and the Mennonite Central Committee. It is a narrative designed to curse Israel and break her economically.

> Last year, the Presbyterian Church (U.S.A.) voted to sell stock in a few companies whose products are used by Israel in the territories. The United Church of Christ resolution was broader. Delegates are calling on the denomination's financial arms to sell off stock

in any company profiting from what the church called human rights violations arising from the occupation. The church also voted to boycott [Israeli] products made in the territories.[125]

The protestors who often act under the concept of BDS have mutated from legitimate concerns to being openly anti-Semitic. Israel has been accused of being an apartheid state akin to South Africa in the mid-twentieth century. The aim of those protesting is the total collapse of Israel. While the tactics are different, the reality is that BDS is no better than the regimes of Iran, Syria, Iraq, and other Arab states desiring to see the annihilation of the State of Israel.

The Word of God is very explicit in the Genesis 12:3 (KJV) admonition, "I [God] will bless them that bless thee"; and in the New Testament book of Luke:

> Give, and it will be given to you. A good measure, pressed down, shaken together and running over, will be poured into your lap. For with the measure you use, it will be measured to you. (Luke 6:38 NIV)

Author and theologian Rev. Simon Ponsonby writes that the church of Jesus Christ today needs to "renew her understanding of her Jewish roots and reach out to the Jews with love and gratitude . . . If we turn our affections on the Jewish people we'll see more of

God's blessings on the church."[126] This determination to stand with the Jewish people would almost certainly bring revival to the church. Then united Believers would be able to "stand against the schemes of the devil" (see Ephesians 6:11 ESV) whose sole determination is to destroy the seed of Abraham.

22

THROUGHOUT THE BIBLE God has made eternal promises to the people of Israel, and the survival of the Jews is a fulfillment of those biblical prophecies. Simply put: Had the Jews not survived, God's Word would not be true!

Jehovah made a covenant with the children of Israel and deeded the land to Abraham, Isaac, and Jacob through *their* descendants—not through Ishmael and *his* descendants. God's covenant promise cannot be broken—not by the Jews' captivity in other nations, not by war, not even by repeated cycles of iniquity and penitence. Ultimately, His chosen ones returned to their land of promise—not because of mandates issued by other countries or the United Nations; it was God's covenant promise being fulfilled!

Across the centuries, a remnant—God's precious seed—has always remained in the promised land. That you and I live in this day and time and have witnessed the scattered Jews returned and restored to their covenant land should be a matter of both wonder and worship for a God who keeps His promises—always:

> For the LORD is good and his gracious love stands forever. His faithfulness remains from generation to generation. (Psalm 100:5 ISV)

The return of the Jews to the promised land following World War II and the revulsion of the Holocaust demanded that the Christian church take a closer look at the Abrahamic covenant. It was a combination of the return and the awfulness of what had been done to the Jewish people in the concentration camps that dealt a deathblow to anti-Semitism in many but, sadly, not all churches.

Christians dare not claim belief in John 3:16, and then disavow scriptures that call for the support of His chosen people. The church must either believe the entire Bible, or none of it. The rebirth of Israel in 1948 was the fulfillment of biblical prophecy. For the church to purposefully close its heart to the cries of God's people is akin to willfully and disdainfully ignoring His precise instructions in the Word.

The fact that the Jewish people exist is a miracle. The rebirth of the nation of Israel was a miracle. The restoration of the Hebrew language, the return of the Jewish people to their homeland, and the reunification of Jerusalem was a wonder. Israel must either be embraced or opposed; one cannot straddle the fence.

Why should Christians stand shoulder to shoulder with the Jewish people and Israel? The answer is simple: because God affirms Israel in His Word! Some Christians have been heard to say disdainfully, "I will not support the Jews in Israel. They are sinners, and the nation is a sinful one." How easy it is to forget the countless mercies God has bestowed on a sinful United States to whom He made not one direct promise. How can we sing, "God Bless America," when this nation leads the world in having murdered a number approaching 60 million babies by abortion since Roe vs. Wade became law, and then curse Israel with a self-righteous attitude? When you do the math, that is approximately the number of total casualties of the Holocaust and World War II combined. Given that Germany faced judgment for its actions in World War II, how then shall the United States escape judgment? Will turning away from Israel be the straw that breaks the camel's back? And if yes, what then awaits America? Will it see more fires, floods, and fierce storms?

True, some in Israel are guilty of the same sins as other secular Western nations—abortion, homosexuality, murder, adultery, and more. However, the promises of God given to the children of Israel through the Old Testament prophets were unconditional. Fulfillment of His prophetical edicts is not reliant upon their belief, submission, or uprightness; it is entirely dependent on God's supreme power and His unchangeable resolve (Isaiah 2:2–5). He promised that after His people were returned to Israel, He would be revealed to them:

"Therefore say: 'This is what the Sovereign LORD says: Although I sent them far away among the nations and scattered them among the countries, yet for a little while I have been a sanctuary for them in the countries where they have gone.'

"Therefore say: 'This is what the Sovereign LORD says: I will gather you from the nations and bring you back from the countries where you have been scattered, and I will give you back the land of Israel again.'

"They will return to it and remove all its vile images and detestable idols. I will give them an undivided heart and put a new spirit in them; I will remove from them their heart of stone and give them a heart of flesh. Then they will follow my decrees and be careful to keep my laws. They will be my people, and I will be their God." (Ezekiel 11:16–20 NIV)

It is the responsibility of believing Christians to pray with and for the Jewish people. John, the brother of Jesus Christ, wrote:

If any one says, "I love God," and hates his brother, he is a liar; for the one who does not love his brother whom he has seen, cannot love God whom he has not seen. (1 John 4:20 RSV)

To summarize the sixty-six books of the Bible in one word, you only have to say "Israel." The Bible begins with and ends with Israel. There is no word used more. There are no promises given to any people more than to Israel. Israel's very existence demonstrates the faithfulness of God, the inspiration and infallibility of the Bible, and the sovereignty of God.

There is a doctrine in vogue spawned in hell, which teaches that the church has replaced Israel in the plans and heart of God. This doctrine is known alternately as replacement theology, progressive dispensationalism, or supersessionism. The early church did not teach this; its roots date back to the European church. This patently false doctrine states that the church has supplanted Israel in God's plan for the ages, and that the Jews have been rejected; that they have been blinded for having crucified Christ. These followers believe Israel failed God and as a result was replaced by the church. It teaches that the church is a spiritual Israel and that Jerusalem is any town in which there is a church.

Replacement theology feeds anti-Semitism through ignorance and lack of understanding. For instance, the Jews have often been labeled "Christ killers" because of the crucifixion. This has led to attacks of every imaginable nature being launched against them. They have constantly faced lack, banishment, attack, or the threat of eradication.

I believe any theological idea that separates Christians from their Jewish roots is unscriptural, with the practical result being that it stunts spiritual understanding and growth. Supersessionism is defined as

> ... the theological concept that, because Judaism did not accept Jesus as their Messiah, God terminated his covenants with the Jewish people and transferred them to the followers of Christianity. It relegates Judaism to an inferior position and recognizes Christianity as the "true" or "spiritual" Israel.[127]

Replacement theology rejects the concept that the promises God made to Israel are for this present hour; that instead, they were canceled at Calvary. As a result, this doctrine contends, these promises now fall to the church, which has replaced Israel. The absurdity of this dogma is that if Christian leaders believe God ended His promises to the Jewish people, they must also believe He might revoke His promises to them as well.

What exactly do supersessionists believe?

- ✧ They tend to be anti-Israel, and therefore do not honor Israel.

- ✧ They tend to be pro-Palestinian.

- ✧ They marginalize Christians who support Israel, even with humanitarian issues.

Obviously, these theologians have abandoned the apostle Paul's teaching to the Romans. He wrote in Romans 11:1–2 (NKJV):

> I say then, has God cast away His people? Certainly not! For I also am an Israelite, of the seed of Abraham, of the tribe of Benjamin. God has not cast away His people whom He foreknew. Or do you not know what the Scripture says of Elijah, how he pleads with God against Israel?

In actuality, Martin Luther was not the first to embrace the doctrine of replacement theology. It was first developed by Justin Martyr (circa AD 100–165) and Irenaeus of Lyon (circa AD 130–200). Origen espoused the theory of allegorization—or the use of a parable to explain an event. For instance, he taught that in the triumphal entry the foal was used to symbolize the New Testament gospel, that the two apostles sent to fetch the colt were representative of humanity.

Doesn't it follow, then, that if the donkey was indicative of the Old Testament, and the foal the New Testament, the Israel of the Old Testament is now the church of the New Testament? Such machinations renounce the literal interpretation of the Bible, and then permit preachers, teachers, or priests to cause the Scriptures to say whatever they wish.

This was largely accepted within the church by the fourth century, and has led to a great deal of persecution of Jews by Christians. Some Protestant reformers, however, began to question this practice by the end of the 1500s. Replacement theology, like other misconceptions, rears its head from time to time in an attempt to disavow the relevance of Israel. Although the Catholic Church reversed its stance on replacement theology in the twentieth century, many conservative Protestant groups still ascribe to this doctrine.

As in earlier centuries, at times the church has been a willing participant in genocide perpetrated against the Jews. From the times of the early Catholic Church to the Crusades, from Martin Luther's Reformation to World War II, the church has sometimes been duplicitous in the terrorizing of Jews.

Embracing replacement theology has led to rampant anti-Semitism in some Christian churches. Jews have continuously faced lack, banishment, violence, or the threat of eradication.

This devious doctrine propagates the age-old practice of blaming the Jews for the world's ills, weighing them in the balance and finding them wanting. It also frees these misled believers from their responsibility to share the good news of the gospel of Jesus Christ with all whom He came to seek and to save, including the Jewish people.

In that the concept of replacement theology is still taught in modern times, I wrote in *The American Prophecies*:

By replacing literal Israel in the Bible with the Church, Christians of the time no longer had to feel any responsibility to the Jews as God's Chosen People. This

"Replacement Theology" would be exactly what would quiet the Church in Germany during World War II as the death camps sped into full swing. They had no obligation to the Jews. They [the Jews] were "suffering for their sins of rejecting the Messiah." It was as if Jesus' death cut them [the Church] free from these people rather than grafted them into their tree. However they saw it, it was this insidious virus—an invisible moderate anti-Semitism—that allowed the . . . Church to look the other way as the most horrific and ungodly things were done.[128]

On the other hand, a 1923 article in the *Pentecostal Evangel* was quick to reassure its readers that the Jews would fulfill God's purpose for Israel—that the love of their homeland had been deeply instilled in the descendants of Abraham, Isaac, and Jacob; that their fervent prayer of "next year in Jerusalem" had echoed throughout the ages; and that God would hear that cry and respond. The article further assured that a tiny shoot of the fig tree was just beginning to break the soil in Palestine and nothing—not the Bishop of Jerusalem, not opposition from the Arabs, not replacement theology or those who were ignorant of God's Word—would hinder His plan for His chosen people.[129]

The prevailing view among those espousing supersessionism—that the church has replaced God's chosen people—is vastly different from the theology taught in the New Testament. The church is totally divergent from Israel—the two are not interchangeable. The church was born on the day of Pentecost; Israel was born of God's covenant with Abraham.

For centuries the evils of replacement theology have resembled a cancer within the body of Christ. The claim that the Jews rejected Christ, therefore all the promises of Abraham were bestowed on the church and all the curses fell upon Israel is a patent error. In recent years, Evangelical Christians have worked diligently to dispel that lie.

When the church tries to replace Israel:

✧ Arrogance and egotism replace love and compassion.

✧ It becomes boastful and complacent.

✧ Both Israel and the Jewish people are diminished.

✧ Anti-Semitism becomes rampant.

✧ Bible prophecies lose their importance and fulfillment is often overlooked.

✧ The Old Testament loses its significance and substance. The Bible of the early church was not the New Testament; rather, it was the Hebrew Scriptures.

Sadly, the church failed from its inception to realize the importance of those truths. Had that not been the case, the anti-Semitism that has plagued it for centuries might have been circumvented. Instead, the church has been infected with the cancer of replacement theology—a very real violation of the Word of God. It has often made the church a repository of hatred rather than love, as it should have been for the past 2,000 years.

In Numbers 23:19 (ESV) we are told of God's infallibility:

> God is not man, that he should lie, or a son of man,
> that he should change his mind. Has he said, and will
> he not do it? Or has he spoken, and will he not fulfill it?

Hebrews 6:18 tells us it is *impossible* for God to lie; and Titus 1:2 states flatly that God *cannot* lie.

If a God who does not and cannot lie made a covenant with the Jewish people, He *will* keep His word.

23

IN ZECHARIAH 2:8 the ancient prophet wrote: "For he who touches you, touches the apple [pupil] of His eye" (NASB). Anti-Semitism is hatred against all Jews. At its very root is arguably hatred of God and His Word. Martin Niemoller, the anti-Nazi theologian and Lutheran pastor wrote:

> First they came for the Socialists,
>
> and I did not speak out—
>
> Because I was not a Socialist.
>
> Then they came for the Trade Unionists,
>
> and I did not speak out—
>
> Because I was not a Trade Unionist.
>
> Then they came for the Jews,
>
> and I did not speak out—
>
> Because I was not a Jew.
>
> Then they came for me—
>
> and there was no one left to speak for me.[130]

Hitler employed the duplicitous and anti-Semitic hoax *The Protocols of the Learned Elders of Zion* to murder six million Jews during World War II. Historian Norman Cohn suggested that Hitler used *The Protocols* as his primary justification for initiating the Holocaust—his "warrant for genocide."[131]

The trend continues today among Arab countries:

> ... in the Middle East, where a large number of Arab and Muslim regimes and leaders have endorsed them as authentic ... The 1988 charter of Hamas, a Palestinian Islamist group, states that *The Protocols of the Elders of Zion* embodies the plan of the Zionists.[132] Recent endorsements in the 21st century have been made by the Grand Mufti of Jerusalem, Sheikh Ekrima Sa'id Sabri, the education ministry of Saudi Arabia, member of the Greek Parliament Ilias Kasidiaris, and young earth creationist and tax protester Kent Hovind.[133]

The appalling historical record reveals that Jewish people have been the targets of fierce discrimination and persecution over countless centuries, both in Islamic countries and even in so-called Christian lands. Vatican-inspired Crusaders systematically murdered Jews during the Middle Ages. The Roman Catholic Inquisitions were directed against the Jews in Spain and elsewhere, leaving many dead or in prison. The pogroms of Russia and Eastern

Europe forced Jews from their homes and left untold numbers slaughtered.

As evil as these anti-Semitic assaults were, they all pale in comparison to the Holocaust of World War II. A full one-third of the entire Jewish race was annihilated by Hitler's Nazi forces. The utter horror of this hellish practice that was the Holocaust as revealed by the testimonies of death-camp survivors cannot be overstressed. Something to which we tend to give little credence is the definition of the term "Nazi." It is often used so wantonly in this day that we forget it has an absolute meaning. It was a term coined by the National Socialist Movement, an organization devoted solely to the most malicious and deadly form of anti-Semitism.

Too late, many Germans recognized the blessings that the Jewish people brought to their society before Hitler's tragic rise to power. Jewish composers, scientists, doctors, teachers, writers, and others contributed their significant talents and intelligence and were callously repaid in Hitler's death chambers.

In the twenty-first century, anti-Semitism continues to raise its ugly head in the unlikeliest of places:

> Belgian Justice Minister Stefaan De Clerck shocked the country's Jewish community by voicing support for an initiative to provide amnesty to Nazi collaborators during WWII, and for his suggestion that it may behoove the

government to "forget" its Nazi past. During a television debate, De Clerck said that the country should not focus on the crimes it committed as it was already in the past.

In fairness there are plenty of crimes being committed now against Belgium's Jews. The country's anti-Semitism is partly why the safety of European Jews is at its lowest since the Second World War, with anti-Jewish attacks at postwar highs. So maybe De Clerck was saying that Belgians should focus on their present anti-Semitism rather than on their past anti-Semitism.[134]

Could this be, I wonder, why Belgium became the focus of the manhunt for accessories to the bloody terrorist attacks that took place in France in November 2015? The violence claimed the lives of at least 130 and wounded more than 350. In a *USA Today* article, journalist Oren Dorrell wrote, "Recruiting network Sharia4Belgium wants to convert Belgium—whose capital of Brussels is also the capital of the European Union—into an Islamic State."[135] Salah Abdeslam, the brother of one of the slain jihadists, was believed to have taken refuge in Belgium.

Unfortunately some say, "I don't need to reach out to the suffering house of Israel. Why, the Bible says there will be wars and rumors of wars over there, until the Messiah comes. It's all part of prophecy." (See Matthew 24:6)

To simply say that there is no need to pray and support the Jewish people, my friend, is anti-Semitic nonsense. It is to say that Nehemiah, Esther, and even our Lord were wrong to pray and reach out in love to the house of Israel. There are hundreds of examples of prophets, priests, and pontiffs who chose to light a candle rather than curse the darkness.

The setting of Isaiah 40 follows the dispersion of the Jewish people to Babylon. The children of Israel had been captives, distraught by the circumstances in which they found themselves. Those left behind in Jerusalem, also ruled by the Babylonians, were equally distressed. As a release for their grief and agitation, the book of Lamentations was written. In Lamentations 1:17 (NLT), the writer records, "Jerusalem reaches out for help, but no one comforts her."

Now in Isaiah chapter 40, change has come: "Comfort, O comfort My people . . . Speak kindly to Jerusalem" (Isaiah 40:1–2 NASB). The Hebrew people have paid the price for their sin, and the time for comfort has come. Professor and theologian John Goldingay wrote of the time:

> The city [of Jerusalem] is like a woman who has lost husband and children and sits desolate like Job on his heap of ashes. She has sat this way for nearly half a century. Now a voice declares Comfort, comfort my people.

The time for the plaint in Lamentations is over. And the one who speaks is **your God**.[136]

The voice heard is not just any voice; it is God's voice. The price has been paid and comfort has come as a result of Israel's repentance, of sighing and lamenting over the cause of their captivity. Jehovah, merciful and gracious, has now sent His Spokesman to offer comfort and consolation. He has sent a Servant to offer tenderness, the balm of Gilead to bind up their wounded spirits and broken hearts. God's response to their repentance is "I am with you. I have neither forgotten nor forsaken you." That theme is repeated again and again throughout the remainder of the book of Isaiah.

The children of Israel had suffered through a terrible calamity. They were in need of comfort, of being assured that their time of catastrophe was coming to an end. It was time for encouragement, for knowing that God had not forsaken them. Darkness had covered the land, but Israel had not been cast aside by Yahweh. The time for restoration was at hand; the time for comfort had come. The God of all comfort had declared it to be a time for consolation.

In his commentary on Isaiah, Old Testament scholar Walter Brueggemann writes:

Enough! Enough sentence, enough penalty, enough payment, enough exile, enough displacement! This is an assertion of forgiveness, but it is not cheap or soft or easy forgiveness. There is, in any case, a limit to the sentence. It can be satisfied and served out. And now it is ended![137]

The prophetic word given by Isaiah was not just for that time; it is a God-given mandate to Christians today to offer comfort, encouragement, and emotional and financial support to the suffering house of Israel. If this Scripture is not for Christians, then for whom is it? Nation after nation has turned its back on the Jewish people. God will not forget those who abandon Israel, just as He will not forget those who reach out in love and assistance. This assignment is echoed in Paul's second letter to the Corinthians:

> Praise be to the God and Father of our Lord Jesus Christ, the Father of compassion and the God of all comfort, who comforts us in all our troubles, so that we can comfort those in any trouble with the comfort we ourselves receive from God. (2 Corinthians 1:3–4 NIV)

The House of Israel seems to have fallen among robbers who have not only stolen their land but their lives. Many people watch with little, if any, concern as Jews again today become scapegoats for the world's inequities. The economy tanks—must be the fault of Jewish bankers. Disease runs rampant—surely was caused by the Jews. Floods, fires, hurricanes, tornadoes, famine—the Jews have to be somehow responsible. Right? That has certainly been the mind-set of Arab leaders for decades.

According to an article in the *Jerusalem Post*, there are as many reasons Arabic-speaking people believe these lies as there are Arabs in the region:

> A Swiss reporter interviewed a high-ranking official in the oil-rich United Arab Emirates and asked why the school system wasn't better. Ah, explained the man, this was all due to Israel.
>
> While the following are generalizations, they are generally true. Arabic-speaking people live in terrible, [closed] societies marked by massive injustice and poor prospects for improvement. Their lives are increasingly governed by restrictions based on religious interpretation, large-scale segregation by gender, a contrast of which they are well aware between the repression and stagnation of their own countries and the relative freedom and progress in other parts of the world. . . .
>
> There is deep resentment of the West for past imperialism, its relative power and wealth and cultural and religious differences.
>
> All of these factors are systematically fed to the masses on a daily basis by mosques, schools, leaders,

opposition politicians, media and just about every other institution.

And yet we are to believe that this problem is entirely or almost entirely caused by Israel's existence, the Arab-Israeli conflict and the situation of the Palestinians. That's it? Why do people say this? One reason is ignorance. The conflict is all they know about the Middle East, and this answer is what they are constantly told by most experts and some media.

Another reason is politics, as it is a talking point by those who for various reasons want to wipe Israel off the map or weaken it. [138]

We in the United States find ourselves at a critical crossroad: Do we believe the God of the Bible and stand with Israel? Or will we turn our backs on the Jewish people and embrace the Liberal Left views of those who commiserate with Israel's enemies? Many Americans embrace the *thought* of religion but have turned their backs on its *reality*—an adherence to the Word of God.

Since 9/11 the United States has been embroiled in a war against radical Islamic groups. Our homeland has been made more vulnerable by the refusal to call a terrorist a terrorist. Those who desire to see the demise of the United States are often referred to erroneously as "freedom fighters." Its presidents over the past few decades have pressed Israel not to retaliate against those fanatics who "only" want to see the Jewish people annihilated. Israel has further been compelled to give up land for peace—a futile exercise. In the entire chapter of Joel 3:1–17, God calls the nations to account for their treatment of His people:

> In those days and at that time, when I restore the fortunes of Judah and Jerusalem, I will gather all nations and bring them down to the Valley of Jehoshaphat. There I will put them on trial for what they did to my inheritance, my people Israel, because they scattered my people among the nations and **divided up my land.** (Emphasis mine, Joel 3:1–2 NIV)

Truthfully, all the world's nations may turn their collective backs on the Jews, but God will never forsake His people:

> For Israel hath not been forsaken, nor Judah of his God, of the LORD of hosts; though their land was filled with sin against the Holy One of Israel. (Jeremiah 51:5 KJV)

24

INTIMIDATED CHRISTIANS in Europe during Hitler's reign maintained their silence while death camps spewed smoke and ashes across the landscape. Once the horrors of German concentration camps became public, people began to understand that the Jews had suffered horribly at the hands of the Nazis, and their living conditions following the end of the war were equally as deplorable. A place of sanctuary was needed for those who had been so horribly abused; change was an absolute necessity. Perhaps a stimulus for any change in some countries was the understanding that if Palestine, the ancient homeland of the Jews, was not opened to Jewish immigration, those survivors would be cast on the mercy of other Western nations.

Once the decision was made to allow the children of Israel to return to their homeland, it was not long before groups such as the National Council of Churches (NCC), now a member of the World

Council of Churches (WCC) founded in 1948, in conjunction with other organizations, began to denigrate the plan for a Jewish homeland in Palestine.

From that day forward, the WCC and its constituent denominational organizations have generally portrayed Israel's behavior as being in lockstep with Arab rhetoric. They believe and declare that all subsequent wars have been fomented by Israel for the purpose of further territorial gain and for the opportunity to incorporate innocent and abject Arab populations. (Ironically, those Arab men, women, and children would benefit far more by being under Israeli administration.)

The WCC pressed constantly through the 1970s and 1980s for America's official contact with the PLO and denounced Israel's punitive responses to terrorism and civil disruption. It denounced the Camp David Accords of 1978 for allegedly ignoring the national ambitions of the "Palestinians." Its consistent line is that "Israel's repeated defiance of international law, its continuing occupation and the impunity it has so long enjoyed are the fundamental causes of the present violence and threaten peace and security of both peoples."[139]

In September 2001, WCC representatives attending the UN Conference on Racism, Racial Discrimination, Xenophobia, and Related Intolerance at Durban, South Africa, infamously led the demand to officially denounce Israel for "systematic perpetration of racist crimes including war crimes, acts of genocide, and ethnic cleansing."[140]

When organizations professing to be comprised of people who believe the Bible to be the Word of God turn their backs on His chosen people, how can its members ever hope to enjoy the blessings promised to those who stand with Israel? The answer again lies in Genesis 12:3, where God promised Abraham that he would curse the individual who cursed Israel. The writer of Proverbs offered this warning: "Then poverty will pounce on you like a bandit; scarcity will attack you like an armed robber." (Proverbs 6:11 NLT)

When it became blatantly apparent in the 1960s that many in Christian churches were turning a blind eye to the plight of the Israelis, Dr. Franklin H. Littell, chairman of the Department of Religion at Temple University, felt the call to confront the church regarding its lack of response to the Nazi-led methodical murder of six million Jews. Dr. Littell was convinced that *"Qui tacet consentit"* (silence implies consent) was unequivocally true. The good doctor was appalled when much of the church again remained silent in the weeks leading up to the Six-Day War. He felt that the lack of response indicated compliance. Dr. Littell wrote that such passivity signaled acquiescence to the Arab mandate that Israel be driven into the sea.

As Israel worked to push back her enemies, Littell worked to resurrect among Protestant churches the spirit of support for the Jewish nation. Following Israel's success on the battlefield, he introduced his new organization, Christians Concerned for Israel (CCI). It was, for Dr. Littell, a testament to the effectiveness of the other pro-Israel organizations that had come before.

In 1978, the CCI became the embryo for the National Christian Leadership Conference of Israel, a much larger group whose foundation was laid during US congressional hearings to authorize the sale of AWACS (Airborne Warning and Control System) to Saudi Arabia. The sale was contested by Prime Minister Begin, as well as senators Edward Kennedy and Bob Packwood. Despite the opposition, the sale of AWACS was finally approved by Congress in October 1981. Christians representing organizations across the United States amassed in Washington, D.C., to protest the sale. Many of the organizers were amazed at the number that responded to show their support for Israel and the determination and emotion that was exhibited.

Even though ridiculed, reviled, and rebuffed by many of the mainline churches, Christian Zionists have continued to support Israel. These dedicated men and women continue to battle anti-Semitism through both the written and spoken word. The support of Evangelicals for the descendants of Abraham, Isaac, and Jacob is genuine and should not be dismissed as irrelevant.

In light of all the biblical evidence presented to this point, it may be safely concluded that Christians have a God-given mandate to honor the Jewish people, wherever they are. But how does this connect to modern Israel? Many Christians seem happy enough to embrace

Jewish neighbors living alongside them in largely Gentile lands but are indifferent or even hostile to the proposition that they also have a duty to support what many see as the controversial State of Israel. Some Believers bristle at the mere suggestion that God has anything to do with Israel's amazing restoration in our era.

Centuries before the Jewish people first were forced into foreign captivity, God revealed that they would be expelled from their covenant land due to sin. But He also promised to eventually restore them to the promised land. This prophecy came via Moses—whose parents came from the tribe of Levi—while he was in the process of boldly leading the children of Israel from the bondage of Egypt into Canaan:

> That the LORD your God will bring you back from captivity, and have compassion on you, and gather you again from all the nations where the LORD your God has scattered you. (Deuteronomy 30:3 NKJV)

This prophecy is not only addressing the return of the Jewish people from Assyrian and Babylonian captivity hundreds of years before the time of Christ. It was ancient Hebrew prophets who also foretold that Israel's loving God would restore His people to their promised land in the last days of history, just before Messiah begins His reign in Jerusalem. This implies that the Jews would be exiled two times from their beloved homeland, which is exactly what has historically taken place.

The prophets also foretold that the final Jewish ingathering would be from all over the globe, unlike the first return from lands directly to the east of Israel. It would be a permanent return, meaning no additional exiles would follow. Most significantly, it would end with the spiritual revival that King Solomon prophesied:

> If My people who are called by My name will humble themselves, and pray and seek My face, and turn from their wicked ways, then I will hear from heaven, and will forgive their sin and heal their land. (2 Chronicles 7:14 NKJV)

There are many prophetic passages about this important topic in the Bible—far too many to quote them all here. But let's take a look at three of them:

> "I will bring back the captives of My people Israel;
> They shall build the waste cities and inhabit them;
> They shall plant vineyards and drink wine from them;
> They shall also make gardens and eat fruit from them.
> I will plant them in their land,
> And no longer shall they be pulled up
> From the land I have given them,'"
> Says the LORD your God. (Amos 9:14–15 NKJV)

"For behold, the days are coming," says the LORD, "'that I will bring back from captivity My people Israel and Judah," says the LORD. "And I will cause them to return to the land that I gave to their fathers, and they shall possess it." (Jeremiah 30:3 NKJV)

Who hath heard such a thing? who hath seen such things? Shall the earth be made to bring forth in one day? or shall a nation be born at once? for as soon as Zion travailed, she brought forth her children. Shall I bring to the birth, and not cause to bring forth? saith the LORD: shall I cause to bring forth, and shut the womb? saith thy God. Rejoice ye with Jerusalem, and be glad with her, all ye that love her: rejoice for joy with her, all ye that mourn for her: That ye may suck, and be satisfied with the breasts of her consolations; that ye may milk out, and be delighted with the abundance of her glory. For thus saith the LORD, Behold, I will extend peace to her like a river, and the glory of the Gentiles like a flowing stream: then shall ye suck, ye shall be borne upon her sides, and be dandled upon her knees. As one whom his mother comforteth, so will I comfort you; and ye shall be comforted in Jerusalem. (Isaiah 66:8–13 KJV)

Nearly half the Jews on earth have now returned to their biblical promised land. Christians worldwide should be exuberant support-ers of this prophesied restoration, for it confirms that the God of Israel does indeed exist, that the prophecies of Bible are true, that He holds the future in His capable hands, that He is a covenant-keeping Lord, and that He is a merciful God who forgives the sins of His people.

Israel was not first born in 1948; she was born in the heart and mind of God and revealed to Abraham many years before the birth of Isaac. God made a blood covenant with Abraham that the land of Canaan would be given to his seed through Isaac (Genesis 15:18). As part of that vision, God told Abraham that for four hundred years his seed would be strangers in a land that did not belong to them (Genesis 15:13). In fulfillment of prophecy, the offspring of Isaac spent four hundred years in Egypt before Moses miraculously led them out, and Israel, the nation, was born.

Unique as this religious centrality is, there is one reason above all others why committed Christians must stand with Israel: The God of the universe, the God that we worship, has chosen to make an *everlasting* covenant with the physical descendants of Abraham, Isaac, and Jacob—the Jewish people.

The word *everlasting* has nothing temporary or conditional about it. It clearly means "lasting forever." Although Jews in number are found today in North and South America, Australia, Asia, Europe, many parts of Africa, and virtually every non-Muslim nation on earth, their historic spiritual and physical center has always been the promised land of Israel.

God's eternal covenant with the descendants of Abraham featured the promise to give them the land of Israel as an everlasting possession. This is recorded in the very first book of the Bible, Genesis, in chapter 17:

> When Abram was ninety-nine years old, the LORD appeared to Abram and said to him, "I am Almighty God; walk before Me and be blameless. And I will make My covenant between Me and you, and will multiply you exceedingly." Then Abram fell on his face, and God talked with him, saying: "As for Me, behold, My covenant is with you, and you shall be a father of many nations. No longer shall your name be called Abram, but your name shall be Abraham; for I have made you a father of many nations. I will make you exceedingly fruitful; and I will make nations of you, and kings shall come from you. And I will establish My covenant between Me and you and your descendants after you in their generations, for an everlasting covenant, to be God to you and your descendants after you. Also I give to you and your descendants after you the land in which you are a stranger, all the land of Canaan, as an everlasting possession; and I will be their God." (Genesis 17:1–8 NKJV)

God reveals in these verses that many peoples would eventually emerge from Abraham's loins, and so it has been. The Arabs, scattered in over twenty countries throughout the Middle East and North Africa, trace their ancestry to the ancient patriarch who traveled to Canaan at God's command from the town of Ur in Chaldea. Their lineage comes through Ishmael, Abraham's son born to Sarah's handmaid, Hagar. However, the Scriptures go on to reveal that the special, eternal land covenant comes through the line of the son of promise, Isaac, his grandson Jacob, and his twelve great-grandsons—the forefathers of the modern Jewish people. This is summarized in Psalm 105:8–11:

> He remembers His covenant forever,
>
> The word which He commanded,
>
> for a thousand generations,
>
> The covenant which He made with Abraham,
>
> And His oath to Isaac,
>
> And confirmed it to Jacob for a statute,
>
> To Israel as an everlasting covenant,
>
> Saying, "To you I will give the land of Canaan
>
> As the allotment of your inheritance." (NKJV)

As we have seen, the belief that God has revoked His solemn covenant with the Jewish people due to their sin and rebellion against Him is widespread in the church today. It is certainly a fact that living peacefully in the land was conditional on obedience to God's holy law.

Jacob's offspring were warned that they would be removed from the land if they disobeyed God's commands. But the Bible also foretells that a Jewish remnant would be restored to the promised land after worldwide exile, as has wonderfully occurred in our day.

The proclamation "next year in Jerusalem" became a part of the Passover Seder during the Middle Ages. It was an expression of the longing of the Jewish people that Jerusalem and the temple be rebuilt. Today, the nation has been reunified under Jewish authority. It is a flourishing and modern city to which Jews of the Diaspora, forced from home and land through the centuries, have returned. In Psalm 137, the Jews carried away to Babylon sat down and wept as they remembered their homeland and the Holy City:

> There on the poplars we hung our harps, for there our captors asked us for songs, our tormentors demanded songs of joy; they said, "Sing us one of the songs of Zion!" How can we sing the songs of the LORD while in a foreign land? If I forget you, Jerusalem, may my right hand forget its skill. May my tongue cling to the roof of my mouth if I do not remember you, if I do not consider Jerusalem my highest joy. (Psalm 137:2–6 NIV)

The captives did not dash their harps against the rocks around them; their musical instruments were suspended from the trees that dotted the landscape, preserved for use in a future time—in the

Holy City. It was symbolic of the hope of their return to Jerusalem when sorrow would be turned into joy, mourning into dancing, ashes exchanged for beauty, and the spirit of heaviness replaced with the garment of praise (see Isaiah 61:3).

Jehovah God preserved a remnant of His people down through the ages despite Satan's attempts to totally annihilate the Israelites. Jehovah-Mephalti—the Lord my Deliverer—declared: "And you who are left in Judah, who have escaped the ravages of the siege, will put roots down in your own soil and grow up and flourish." (Isaiah 37:31 NLT)

Despite Satan's tactics, he cannot halt God's blessings on His chosen people.

THE AUTHOR of Psalm 121 recorded God's faithfulness to His people:

> Behold, He who keeps Israel
>
> Shall neither slumber nor sleep.
>
> The LORD is your keeper;
>
> The LORD is your shade at your right hand.
>
> The sun shall not strike you by day,
>
> Nor the moon by night.
>
> The LORD shall preserve you from all evil;
>
> He shall preserve your soul.
>
> The LORD shall preserve your going out
>
> and your coming in
>
> From this time forth,
>
> and even forevermore.
>
> Psalm 121:4–8 NKJV

God has not permitted any power to totally exterminate the Jews, although no one people has been plagued, persecuted, pursued, and pressured more throughout their history. Many attempts at annihilation have been made, but all have ended in utter failure, defeat, and humiliation.

Author George Gilder wrote:

> In *Dialogues and Secrets with Kings*, published after the 1967 war, the very first official . . . PLO leader, Ahmad Shuqeiri [said], "I frequently called upon Arabs to liquidate the state of Israel and to throw the Jews into the sea. I said this because I was—and still am—convinced that there is no solution other than the elimination of the state of Israel." [141]

Take a step back in time and look at Egypt and Pharaoh's edict concerning the Israelites:

> So Pharaoh commanded all his people, saying, "Every son who is born you shall cast into the river, and every daughter you shall save alive." (Exodus 1:22 NKJV)

Following Pharaoh's brutal treatment of the children of Israel, God sent Moses to deliver His people from their harsh existence under the Egyptian ruler. In order to change the heart of Pharaoh,

God sent a series of ten plagues against the captors—each targeting one of the false gods worshiped by the Egyptians. The first three curses affected the comfort of the Egyptian people. By turning the water to blood, He denied them what was needed for cleansing and drinking. The Nile River, Hapi, god of the Nile, also worshiped as the giver of life, became instead an agent of death. Second, their homes were invaded with frogs (Heka, god of fertility). (I have never been able to understand why, as Moses asked Pharaoh when he would like to be rid of the frogs, he said, "Tomorrow." Why did he want to spend another night with the slimy, green amphibians?) Third, lice invaded the land Geb (god of the earth), attacking the Egyptians.

When Pharaoh continued to refuse to let God's people go, a second trifecta of plagues was unleashed on the land. They targeted Egypt's false gods. The fourth plague was that of flies, perhaps to let it be known that one of their gods, Beelzebub, lord of the flies, was incapable of rescuing them from Jehovah's wrath. The fifth plague decimated their herds of cattle. Again Jehovah proved He was greater than Apis, the sacred bull worshiped by the Egyptians (and, perhaps, the motivation for the golden calf fashioned in the wilderness). The sixth challenged the claims of Egyptian medical shamans by causing a horrific outbreak of incurable boils (Isis, goddess of medicine). Still, Pharaoh was not moved to release the people to Moses, God's chosen leader.

The last set of three plagues was designed to bring death and desolation as hail rained down on the land, flattening crops and killing more cattle (Nut, goddess of the sky). That was followed by a plague of locusts that stripped any green vegetation remaining after the hailstorms (Seth, god of crops). Then darkness descended upon the land (Ra, the sun god)—so comprehensive that the Bible says:

> During all that time the people could not see each
> other, and no one moved. But there was light as usual
> where the people of Israel lived. (Exodus 10:23 NLT)

In Carlsbad Caverns, New Mexico, at one point during the tour below ground, the guide asks everyone to sit. The lights are then turned off in the huge room for a few moments, and the darkness is complete. You literally cannot see your hand held in front of your face. Imagine: God caused just such a blackness to cover the land of Egypt for three long days. Not a chariot moved; not a shaman prognosticated; no fisherman cast a net, and no merchant plied his trade.

With a still-obstinate Pharaoh refusing to heed the warnings of Moses, God brought forth the tenth and final plague: the death of all the firstborn in Egypt—at least among those not safely hidden beneath the blood covering of the Passover Lamb.

Theologian Arthur W. Pink wrote of the tenth plague:

One more judgment was appointed, the heaviest of them all, and then not only would Pharaoh let the people go, but he would thrust them out. Then would be clearly shown the folly of fighting against God. Then would be fully demonstrated the uselessness of resisting Jehovah. Then would be made manifest the impotence of the creature and the omnipotence of the Most High.[142]

Moses was vitally aware of what was about to befall the Egyptian people. As a baby he was saved by Pharaoh's daughter because of an edict that demanded the deaths of all male babies born to the women of Israel. The king's disobedience would exact a dire penalty not only upon his household but also upon each individual in the land of Egypt. Harsh, yes, but Pharaoh had been given numerous opportunities to heed the voice of Jehovah. Because He is a God of love, a way was made for the Israelites to escape the sentence of death that had been pronounced, but the Egyptians chose instead to ignore the warnings—all ten in the form of the various plagues visited upon the land.

The ruler who had so persecuted the children of Abraham, Isaac, and Jacob, who had ordered every Hebrew male child tossed into the Nile River, lost every eldest son in the land—including his own. For some families, it might have meant the death of every male in the household—grandfather, father, eldest son, grandson. An angry, bitter

Pharaoh gathered his terrified, demoralized troops, and pursued the Hebrew children as they departed Egypt. He led his army directly into the path of God's wrath, and all drowned in the Red Sea. Overnight, Egypt became a land of poverty and disease. It remains that way four thousand years later . . . because it chose to curse the Jewish people rather than bless them.

But Jehovah God didn't stop there: While pursuing the Hebrew children into the wilderness the entire Egyptian army was drowned in the Red Sea as Pharaoh watched helplessly from his chariot overlooking the body of water. God had inexorably triumphed over the enemy of His children:

> Then Moses and the children of Israel sang this song
> to the LORD, and spoke, saying:
>
> "I will sing to the LORD,
> For He has triumphed gloriously!
> The horse and its rider
> He has thrown into the sea!" (Exodus 15:1 NKJV)

The Old Testament book of Esther paints a beautiful picture of God's deliverance of the Jews from the menace of anti-Semitism. Esther, a beautiful young Jewish girl, was torn from her home and taken captive to the palace. There, a tyrannical ruler had banished his queen from the royal throne and initiated a search for her successor.

The king was captivated by Esther and chose her to be his new queen. As in any high drama, there was also a dastardly villain, Haman, who desired to perpetrate genocide against her Jewish people.

> Then Haman said to King Ahasuerus, "There is a certain people scattered and dispersed among the people in all the provinces of your kingdom; their laws are different from all other people's, and they do not keep the king's laws. Therefore it is not fitting for the king to let them remain." (Esther 3:8 NKJV)

Esther's uncle, Mordecai, challenged Esther to approach the king (a move that could have been punishable by death) and ask for the salvation of her people. In encouraging her to do so, Mordecai confronted Esther with these timeless words:

> For if you remain completely silent at this time, relief and deliverance will arise for the Jews from another place, but you and your father's house will perish. Yet who knows whether you have come to the kingdom for such a time as this? (Esther 4:14 NKJV)

Esther's response to Mordecai was magnificent in its faith:

> Go, gather all the Jews who are present in Shushan, and fast for me; neither eat nor drink for three days, night

or day. My maids and I will fast likewise. And so I will
go to the king, which is against the law; and if I perish, I
perish! (Esther 4:16 NKJV)

With great trepidation, Esther approached King Ahasuerus. Miraculously, he granted her an audience. The plan for the destruction of the Jews by the foul villain, Haman, was thwarted, and the king issued a decree throughout the land allowing Esther's people to defend themselves if attacked. Because of this decree, the Jews overcame every enemy and lived in peace (see Esther 8–9). Yet another attempt by Satan to annihilate the Jews was foiled.

Another major example was Satan's endeavor to destroy the Jews during World War II. Germany's leader, Adolf Hitler, declared the Jews were not the chosen people; the Aryan race was. He determined to resolve what he called the "Jewish problem," and disseminated the belief that the Jewish people were responsible for anarchy, dishonesty, and the ruin of civilization, government, and finance. According to those so-called "learned men," the purpose of the Jew was to completely weaken Germany and dilute the superior Aryan race.

The mustachioed little man mesmerized his listeners with a gravelly, impassioned voice—never mind that his speeches contained little of actual value. Near the end of 1921, he had come to be known as the der Führer ("the Leader"). History reveals that Adolf Hitler and his "Final Solution" was responsible for the deaths of six million Jewish men, women, and children while the world turned a blind eye to his determination to destroy. This "hide your head in the sand" attitude allowed Hitler, the Nazi Party and its minions to fabricate a massive falsehood against the Jewish people.

The preservation of a remnant of Jews through all the suffering, wars, and afflictions over the centuries is further evidence that Israel and the Jewish people are God's miracle. Our God keeps His covenants; He remains faithful even when we are faithless (see 2 Timothy 2:13). It is He who has sovereignly decided to preserve the Jewish people as a separate, identifiable people before Him and then to restore them to their biblical homeland. These truths are revealed in numerous scriptures. That they would remain on earth until the end of time as a distinct people group is foretold in Jeremiah 31:

> Thus says the LORD,
>
> Who gives the sun for a light by day,
>
> The ordinances of the moon
>
>   and the stars for a light by night,
>
> Who disturbs the sea,
>
> And its waves roar
>
> (The Lord of hosts is His name):
>
> "If those ordinances depart
>
> From before Me, says the LORD,
>
> Then the seed of Israel shall also cease

From being a nation before Me forever."

(Jeremiah 31:35–36 NKJV)

The next verse makes it crystal clear that the God of Abraham has no intention of ever forsaking His special covenant with Jacob's children, despite many failures:

> I will direct their work in truth,
>
> And will make with them an everlasting covenant.
>
> Their descendants shall be known among the Gentiles,
>
> And their offspring among the people.
>
> All who see them shall acknowledge them,
>
> That they are the posterity whom the Lord
>
> has blessed. (Isaiah 61:8–9 NKJV)

God calls the land of Israel "My land" (Ezekiel 38:16), and He gave it to Israel through a blood covenant that cannot be annulled. God has assigned the land of Israel to the children of Israel, and has never cancelled that which He assigned.

God said that Israel *would* be scattered among the heathen, and they *were*. The Enemy must have thought surely that his plan was working. God also said they would be regathered, and they have been.

AFTERWORD

IN 2012, I TRAVELED to Jerusalem to seek a location for the Friends of Zion (FOZ) Museum in the Holy City. Through the museum, the accounts of Christians who played a crucial role in helping to promote, defend, support, and establish the modern state of Israel would be told, as would the stories of those men and women who fulfilled their moral duty to rescue Jewish people from the Holocaust. Today the attractive building that houses the museum sits in the heart of Jerusalem at 20 and 22 Yosef Rivlin Street, a prominent location overlooking Independence Park and within walking distance of the Old City.

My heart overflows with gratitude to God as the fulfillment of a dream He placed in my spirit more than thirty years ago has become a reality. It is one more building block in the plan and purpose God has surely had for my life. The Friends of Zion Heritage Center (FOZ), a $100-million project in Jerusalem gained ten million members in its first year of operation. FOZ, just six hundred meters from the Temple Mount, is ground zero for the global Jerusalem Prayer Team prayer movement. With over one billion Christian Zionists worldwide, the goal is to unite them to stand with Israel and the Jewish people. FOZ now has a vast social network platform to mobilize Israel's greatest friends worldwide. The organization already has more than one million members in Indonesia alone, and is presently growing by a staggering two million members monthly. A massive communication hub has been planned to link to the thousands of Christian television and radio outlets globally, as well as to churches and universities.

For decades, sympathetic Gentiles from around the world have joined Jewish people in the trenches. With each succeeding battle for existence, new Bible-believing Christians have sprung up to stand with the children of Israel in their struggle to survive. These are the men and women who are spotlighted in the new Museum of Christian Zionism in Jerusalem—those who have staunchly supported the Jewish people before, during, and after the rebirth of Israel.

When the contract for the purchase of the building that houses the Friends of Zion Heritage was signed, I was reminded once again that every promise from God is certain and sure, no matter how long we have to wait for it.

Abraham waited for the promised birth of Isaac for some twenty-five years, but in God's perfect timing, the son of promise was born. When I first met with Prime Minister Menachem Begin more than thirty years ago and we agreed to work together to build a bridge between Christians and Jews, part of that dream was to have a permanent presence in the Holy City. Now we proudly point to this beautiful facility that ministers to the Jewish people and to Christians worldwide.

There is a God-given, biblical—and intimate—connection between Christians and Jews. Based on love and truth, and surrounded by prayer, it can never be broken.

ENDNOTES

1. Eric R. Mandel, "Is the United Nations Anti-Semitic?" *The Jerusalem Post*, July 7, 2014, http://www.jpost.com/Opinion/Op-Ed-Contributors/Is-the-United-Nations-anti-Semitic-361842; accessed November 2016.

2. Elli Wohlgelernter, "One Day that Shook the World," *The Jerusalem Post*, 30 April 1998; https://en.wikipedia.org/wiki/Israeli_Declaration_of_Independence#cite_note-JPost-16; accessed October 2016.

3. "Ancient Wall Possibly built by King Solomon," LiveScience, February 22, 2010, https://www.livescience.com/9828-ancient-wall-possibly-built-king-solomon.html' accessed March 2017.

4. "Ten Top Discoveries," *Biblical Archaeology Review*, July/August/September/October 2009; http://www.bib-arch.org/bar/article.asp?PubID=BSBA&Volume=35&Issue=4&ArticleID=15; accessed July 2010.

5. "Archaeological Discoveries: Artifacts from Temple Mount Saved from Garbage," http://www.jewishvirtuallibrary.org/artifacts-from-temple-mount-saved-from-garbage-october-2005; accessed July 2017.

6. Mark Ami-El, "The Destruction of the Temple Mount Antiquities," *Jerusalem Center for Public Affairs*, August 1, 2002; http://jcpa.org/jl/vp483.htm; accessed July 2010.

7. "Articles," *City of David: Ancient Jerusalem*; http://www.cityofdavid.org.il/Articles_eng.asp?id=64; accessed July 2010.

8. Douglas Helms, "Walter Lowdermilk's Journey: Forester to Land Conservationist," NRCS History Articles, Reprinted from *Environmental Review* 8(1984): 132–145. This paper was given at "History of Sustained-Yield Forestry: A Symposium," at the Western Forestry Center in Portland, Oregon, on October 18–19, 1983, coordinated by the Forest History Society for the International Union of Forestry Research Organizations (IUFRO) Forest Group (S6.07). The proceedings, edited by Harold K. Steen under the same title, were published by the Forest History Society, 109 Coral Street, Santa Cruz, CA 95060, in 1984. http://www.nrcs.usda.gov/about/history/articles/walterlowdermilk.html; accessed January 2011.

9. "The Patriarchs and the Origins of Judaism," *Judaism 101*; http://www.jewfaq.org/origins.htm; accessed April 2012.

10. Ray C. Stedman, *Friend of God: The Legacy of Abraham, Man of Faith* (Grand Rapids, MI: Discovery House Publishers, 2010), 12–13.

11. Genesis 22:6–7 nkjv.

12. Deuteronomy 34:1–4 nkjv.

13. J. L. Robb, "Israel the End Times Prophecies," quoting Charles Krauthammer from *The Weekly Standard*, May 11, 1998, http://www.omegaletter.com/articles/articles.asp?ArticleID=7235; accessed October 2016.

14. "Agrippa I (10 B.C.E.–44 C.E.)," *Jewish Virtual Library*, http://www.jewishvirtuallibrary.org/jsource/judaica/ejud_0002_0001_0_00542.html; accessed August 2015.

15. Michael Farquhar, *A Treasury of Royal Scandals* (New York: Penguin Books, 2001), 209.

16. Flavius Josephus, *Antiquities*, 15, 403 ff. http://www.templemount.org/destruct2.html#anchor596423; accessed July 2017.

17. Ray C. Stedman, *What's This World Coming To?* (An expository study of Matthew 24–26, the Olivet Discourse), (Palo Alto, CA: Discovery Publications, 1970), http://www.templemount.org/destruct2.html#anchor615789; accessed July 2017.

18. Senator Jim Inhofe, "Israel's Right to the Land," http://www.aish.com/h/iid/48891682.html; accessed January 2017.

19. Michael Bar-Zohar, *Ben-Gurion: A Biography* (Jerusalem: Keter, 1989), 18; translated from Hebrew.

20. David Hulme, "David Ben-Gurion: For the Love of Zion," http:// www.vision.org/visionmedia/biography-david-ben-gurion/5810. aspx; accessed June 2017.

21. Gilead Sher, "Ben Gurion: A Political Life," January 6, 2012, https://www.thejc.com/culture/books/ben-gurion-a-political-life-1.30963; accessed June 2017.

22. https://en.wikipedia.org/wiki/Peel_Commission; accessed May 2017.

23. David Hulme, "David Ben-Gurion: For the Love of Zion," http:// www.vision.org/visionmedia/biography-david-ben-gurion/5810. aspx; accessed June 2017.

24. Ibid.

25. William L. Shirer, *The Rise and Fall of the Third Reich*, (New York, NY: Simon and Schuster, 1988), 10–11.

26. John Toland, *Adolf Hitler: The Definitive Biography* (London: Book Club Associates, 1977), 116.

27. Robert Solomon Wistrich, *Who's Who in Nazi Germany* (Hove, East Sussex, UK: Psychology Press, 2002), 118.

28. Houston Stewart Chamberlain, *Letters* (1882–1924 and correspondence with Emperor Wilhelm II) (Munich: F. Bruckmann, 1928), 24. (Translated from the German by Alexander Jacob.)

29. "Adolf Hitler," *Deutsche Presse*, April 20–12, 1944, 1.

30. Deborah E. Lipstadt, *Beyond Belief: The American Press and the Coming of the Holocaust, 1933–1945* (New York: Simon and Schuster, 1993), 79–80.

31. Raul Hilberg, *The Destruction of the European Jews* (New York, NY: Holmes and Meier, 1985), 7f.

32. "The 'Final Solution': The Wannsee Conference," *Jewish Virtual Library*; http://www.jewishvirtuallibrary.org/the-wannsee-conference; accessed March 2017.

33. Victoria J. Barnett, "The Role of the Churches in Nazi Germany: Compliance and Confrontation," http://archive.adl.org/braun/dim_14_1_role_church.html#.Vl8M4f2FM3E; accessed December 2015.

34. Laurel Leff, "How the NYT Missed the Story of the Holocaust While It Was Happening," *George Mason University's History News Network*, April 4, 2005; http://hnn.us/articles/10903.html; accessed March 2017.

35. Walter Laqueur, *The History of Zionism* (London: L.P. Tauris & Co. Ltd, 2003), 557.

36. Golda Meir, *My Life* (NY: Dell, 1975), 213, 222, 224.

37. "Israel Wars & Maps," www.unitedjerusalem.org/HISTORICAL_PERSPECTIVES/Israel_Wars_Maps___History/israel_wars_maps___history.asp; accessed June 2017.

38. Richard H. Curtiss, "Truman Adviser Recalls May 14, 1948, US Decision to Recognize Israel," *Information Clearing House*; http://www.informationclearinghouse.info/article4077.htm; accessed November 2016.

39. "The Recognition of the State of Israel," Truman Library, Eliahu Epstein to Harry S. Truman with attachments re: recognition of Israel, May 14, 1948.

40. Ibid.

41. Ibid.

42. Akhbar al-Yom (Egypt), (October 11, 1947); translated by R. Green, "Interview with Abd al-Rahman Azzam Pasha," *Jewish Virtual Library*; accessed June 2017.

43. Security Council Official Records, SA/Agenda/77 (May 29, 1948), 2.

44. "Modern History of Israel: the Assassination of Count Bernadotte (September 17, 1948)"; http://www.jewishvirtuallibrary.org/the-assassination-of-count-bernadotte; accessed June 2017.

45. Howard Sachar, *A History of Israel*, (NY: Alfred A. Knopf, 1979), 345.

46. Ibid., 452.

47. "Jerusalem," http://en.wikipedia.org/wiki/Jerusalem; accessed March 2013.

48. Simon Sebag Montefiore, *Jerusalem: The Biography* (London, England: Weidenfeld & Nicolson, an imprint of The Orion Publishing Group, 2011), 481–482.

49. "Law of Return," *Jewish Virtual Library*; http://www.jewishvirtuallibrary.org/jsource/Immigration/Text_of_Law_of_Return.html; accessed February 2017.

50. "Ethiopia Virtual Jewish Tour," *Jewish Virtual Library*; http://www.jewishvirtuallibrary.org/jsource/Judaism/ejhist.html; accessed February 2013.

51. "Immigration to Israel: Introduction & Overview," *Jewish Virtual Library*; http://www.jewishvirtuallibrary.org/jsource/Immigration/immigration.html; accessed January 2017.

52. Martin Gilbert, *Israel: A History* (London: Harper Perennial, 2008), 312.

53. "Suez Crisis," *GlobalSecurity.org*; http://www.globalsecurity.org/military/ops/suez.htm; accessed June 2017.

54. Gilbert, 313.

55. Ibid., 324.

56. Ibid., 325.

57. Colonel Richard Meinertzhagen, *Middle East Diary*, (Plainsboro, NJ: Thomas Yoseloff; First Edition,1960), 332.

58. "Golda Meir 1898–1978," *Israel & Judaism Studies*; http://www. ijs.org.au/Golda-Meir/default.aspx; accessed June 2017.

59. Nawaf E. Obaid, "Improving U.S. Intelligence Analysis on the Saudi Arabian Decision-Making Process," (Master's Thesis, John F. Kennedy School of Government, Harvard University, 1998), 13 in Gold, *Hatred's Kingdom*, 60.

60. Gilbert, 327–328.

61. Ibid., 366–367.

62. "The Six-Day War: A Country Study of Egypt," *Jewish Virtual Library*; http://www.jewishvirtuallibrary.org/jsource/History/ LC1967Egypt.html; accessed March 2011.

63. Albert Mohler, "Books for the Backpack," http://www. albertmohler.com/2007/07/18/books-for-the-backpack-recommended-summer-reading-2/; accessed April 2017.

64. Paul Johnson, *A History of the Jews* (New York: harper and Rowe, Publishers, 1987), 537.

65. Abraham Rabinovich, *The Yom Kippur War* (New York: Schocken Books, 2004), 21.

66. "The 1970 Palestinian Hijackings of Three Jets to Jordan, Jets Are Blown Up in the Jordanian Desert," http://middleeast.about. com/od/terrorism/a/dawson-field-hijackings.htm; accessed January 2017.

67. "Jordan asked Nixon to attack Syria, declassified papers show," *CNN Politics,* November 28, 2007; http://www.cnn.com/2007/POLITICS/11/28/nixon.papers/; accessed May 2017.

68. Ibid.

69. Ibid.

70. Simon Dunstan & Kevin Lyles, *The Yom Kippur War 1973: The Sinai* (Westminster, MD: Random House, 2003), 17.

71. Seymour M. Hersh, *The Samson Option: Israel's Nuclear Arsenal and American Foreign Policy* (New York: Vintage Books, 1991), 223.

72. Gilbert, 439.

73. Ibid., 441.

74. Seymour M. Hersh, *The Price of Power: Kissinger in the Nixon White House* (New York: Summit Books, 1983), 234.

75. Johnson, 535.

76. "President Ford Pardons Richard Nixon," *Watergate.info*; http://watergate.info/1974/09/08/ford-pardons-nixon.html; accessed January 2017.

77. Lewis Sorley, *Arms Transfers Under Nixon: A Policy Analysis* (Lexington, KY: University Press of Kentucky, 1983), 193–194.

78. Taken from Tamar Sternthal's report, *"International Herald Tribune* Op-Ed Erases 20-Plus Years of Terror," http://www.camera.org/index.asp?x_context=2&x_outlet=139&x_article=751; accessed February 2017.

79. Johnson, 579–580.

80. *SPIEGEL* Interview with Author David Grossman: "Foreigners Cannot Understand the Israelis' Vulnerability," August 10, 2009, http://www.spiegel.de/international/world/spiegel-interview-with-author-david-grossman-foreigners-cannot-understand-the-israelis-vulnerability-a-641437.html; accessed January 2017.

81. Cited by William F. Jasper in "PLO: Protected Lethal Organization; Despite their terrorist track record, Yasser Arafat the PLO are not only protected from punishment, but are warmly welcomed at the UN," February 11, 2002; http://bit.ly/2BMH7sr; accessed June 2017.

82. Martin, 498.

83. Yitzhak Shamir, "The Failure of Diplomacy," *Israel's Strike Against the Iraqi Nuclear Reactor 7 June, 1981*, Jerusalem: Menachem Begin Heritage Center: 2003, 13–14.

84. "The Strange Side of Jewish History," *Yated Neeman's Jewish History*, http://strangeside.com/israel-atom-bomb-program-part-2-iraq/; accessed June 2017.

85. Louis Rene Beres and Tsiddon-Chatto, Col. (res.) Yoash, "Reconsidering Israel's Destruction of Iraq's Osiraq Nuclear Reactor," *Temple International and Comparitive Law Journal* 9(2), 1995. Reprinted in *Israel's Strike Against the Iraqi Nuclear Reactor 7 June, 1981*, Jerusalem: Menachem Begin Heritage Center: 2003, 60.

86. Maj. Gen. (res.) David Ivry, "The Attack on the Osiraq Nuclear Reactor – Looking Back 21 Years Later," *Israel's Strike Against the Iraqi Nuclear Reactor 7 June, 1981*, Jerusalem: Menachem Begin Heritage Center: 2003, 35.

87. Barbara Walters, *Audition* (New York: Random House, 2008), 350.

88. William F. Jasper, "PLO: Protect Lethal Organization," http://www.freerepublic.com/focus/news/623230/posts; accessed June 2017.

89. R.C. Longworth, "Schultz Helps Arafat Get Right Words," *Chicago Tribune*, December 15, 1988; accessed June 2017

90. Gilbert, 540–542.

91. "The Arab/Muslim World: The Gulf War," http://www.jewishvirtuallibrary.org/the-gulf-war; accessed March 2017.

92. "Oslo II Agreement," September 28, 1995, http://www.acpr.org.il/resources/oslo2.html; accessed December 2016.

93. Richard Miniter, *Losing bin Laden: How Bill Clinton's Failures Unleashed Global Terror* (Washington, DC: Regnery Publishing, Inc., 2003), xvi, xix. (Insert added.)

94. White House Report, "Clinton on life, career, decisions," *Washington File*, August 11, 2000; http://wfile.ait.org.tw/wf-archive/2000/000811/epf501.htm; accessed November 2016.

95. Alan Dershowitz, *What Israel Means to Me* (Hoboken, New Jersey: John Wiley & Sons, Inc., 2006), 53.

96. Jeremy Sutton, "Song for Peace," http://jeremysutton.com/rabin; accessed July 2017.

97. "Yitzhak Rabin: Eulogies at Rabin's Funeral (November 6, 1995)," http://www.jewishvirtuallibrary.org/eulogies-at-the-funeral-of-yitzhak-rabin; accessed July 2017.

98. Gilbert, 593.

99. David Makovsky, "The Silent Strike," *The New Yorker*, September 17, 2012, http://www.washingtoninstitute.org/uploads/Documents/opeds/Makovsky20120917-NewYorker.pdf; accessed July 2017.

100. "The Future of the U.S. Military and Irregular Warfare," Center for Strategic and International Studies, November 22, 2005, http://csis.org/event/future-us-military-and-irregular-warfare; accessed April 2013.

101. http://www.jpost.com/Opinion/An-attack-on-a-Syrian-reactor-504735 ; accessed September 2017.

102. "Police raid publisher over Olmert's secret info leak," https://www.timesofisrael.com/police-raid-publisher-in-follow-up-to-olmerts-secret-information-leak/, June 15, 2017; accessed June 2017

103. David Makovsky, "The Silent Strike," *The New Yorker*, September 17, 2012, http://www.washingtoninstitute.org/uploads/Documents/opeds/Makovsky20120917-NewYorker.pdf; accessed July 2017.

104. "The Covenant of the Islamic Resistance Movement," The Avalon Project: Documents in Law, History and Diplomacy. Yale Law School. 18 August 1988. Retrieved 15 February 2017.

105. Laura Reston, https://newrepublic.com/minutes/123909/world-leaders-have-taken-to-calling-isis-daesh-a-word-the-islamic-state-hates; accessed, July 3017.

106. Ian Schwartz, "Netanyahu on ISIS & Iran: 'The Enemy Of Your Enemy Is Your Enemy," https://www.realclearpolitics.com/video/2015/03/03/netanyahu_on_isis__iran_the_enemy_of_your_enemy_is_your_enemy.html; accessed July 2017.

107. "Iran will NOT develop a nuclear weapon': Obama insists deal with Tehran will work as he promises to veto any legislation to stop it, http://www.dailymail.co.uk/news/article-3160667/This-deal-offers-opportunity-new-direction-seize-President-Obama-speaks-historic-Iran-nuclear-weapons-agreement.html; accessed March 2015.

108. Herb Kinon, "Netanyahu says Iran nuclear deal 'a bad mistake of historic proportions", *Jerusalem Post*, July 14, 2015, http://www.jpost.com/Israel-News/Politics-And-Diplomacy/Netanyahu-says-Iran-nuclear-deal-a-bad-mistake-of-historic-proportions-408895; accessed July 2017.

109. Joel Gehrke, "State Department: Iran Deal Is Not 'Legally Binding' and Iran Didn't Sign It," *National Review*, November 24, 2015, http://www.nationalreview.com/article/427619/state-department-iran-didnt-sign-iran-deal-joel-gehrke; accessed July 2017.

110. Michael Wilner, "JCPOA Anniversary: Has Iran Complied With the Nuclear Deal?" *The Jerusalem Post*, July 8, 2016, http://www.jpost.com/International/JCPOA-Anniversary-Has-Iran-complied-with-the-nuclear-deal-459819; accessed July 2017.

111. Jason Diamond, "The 50 Most Essential Works Of Jewish Fiction Of The Last 100 Years," *Jewcy*, February 9, 2011, http://jewcy.com/jewish-arts-and-culture/books/essential_jewish_fiction; accessed July 2017.

112. Irwin N. Graulich, "Why America Supports Israel," *FrontPageMag.com*, December 20, 2002; http://archive.frontpagemag.com/readArticle.aspx?ARTID=20579; accessed July 2017.

113. Paul Goldman, "Dying 4-year-old girl finds life-savers in the land of the enemy," http://www.saveachildsheart.com/wp-content/uploads/2014/02/2013-05_NBC-News-Dying-4-year-old-girl-finds-life-savers-in-land-of-the-enemy.pdf, May 2013; accessed June 2017.

114. David Miller, "Intelligent 'Wrapping Paper' Heals Broken Bones in Half the Time," December 31, 2013; http://news.yahoo.com/blogs/this-could-be-big-abc-news/intelligent-wrapping-paper-heals-broken-bones-half-time-190710297.html?vp=1; accessed July 2017.

115. Marcella Rosen, "65 years of innovations from Israel," May 9, 2013, *The Jewish Observer*, http://jewishobservernashville. org/2013/05/09/65-years-of-innovations-from-israel/; accessed June 2017.

116. See the full list of innovations and inventions at http:// jewishobservernashville.org/2013/05/09/65-years-of-innovations-from-israel/.

117. "Nobel Prize in Literature 2002," Nobel Foundation; accessed June 2017.

118. "The Nobel Peace Prize for 1986: Elie Wiesel," *Nobelprize.org*, 14 October 1986; accessed June 2017.

119. Hilary Leila Krieger, "He's Got Game," *The Jerusalem Post*, November 1, 2005, http://www.jpost.com/Features/Hes-got-game; accessed June 2017.

120. "Robert Aumann," http://en.wikipedia.org/wiki/Robert_ Aumann; accessed June 2017.

121. http://www.quotationcollection.com/author/Ernest-Hemingway/quotes; accessed June 2017.

122. Karen Ridder, "Israel Boycott: 6 Celebrities Who Have Spoken Against Nation," *Newsmax*, http://www.newsmax.com/ FastFeatures/israel-boycott-celebrities-against/2014/10/29/ id/601979/#ixzz3fyxzk2AM; accessed July 2017.

123. Reuven Rivlin, "Taking Down BDS," *Ynet News*, March 28, 2016, http://www.ynetnews.com/articles/0,7340,L-4784050,00.html; accessed July 2017.

124. Euge rovich, "Is the International Criminal Court biased against Israel?" *The Washington Post*, January 5, 2015, https://www. washingtonpost.com/news/volokh-conspiracy/wp/2015/01/05/ is-the-international-criminal-court-biased-against-israel/?utm_ term=.933f3eb446f6; accessed July 2017.

125. "United Church of Christ to divest over Israeli policies in occupied Palestinian territories," *Star Tribune*, June 30, 2015, http://www.startribune.com/ucc-church-to-divest-over-israeli-treatment-of-palestinians/310966861/; accessed December 2016.

126. "Church must repent of sin of anti-Semitism," Assist News Service, July 16, 2013, http://www.christiantoday.com/article/church.must.repent.of.sin.of.anti.semitism/33198.htm; accessed July 2017.

127. *babylon.com*, Free Online Dictionary; http://www.babylon.com/definition/Supercession/English; accessed June 2017.

128. Michael D. Evans, *The American Prophecies: Ancient Scriptures Reveal our Nation's Future* (New York, NY: Warner Faith, 2004), 55–56.

129. "Here and There," *Pentecostal Evangel*, August 18, 1923, 8.

130. Martin Niemöller: "First They Came for the Socialists..." http://www.ushmm.org/wlc/en/article.php?ModuleId=10007392; accessed October 2016.

131. Cohn, Norman (1966), *Warrant for Genocide: The Myth of the Jewish World Conspiracy and the Protocols of the Elders of Zion* (New York: Harper & Row, 2006), 32–36.

132. "Hamas Covenant," Yale, 1988: "Today it is Palestine, tomorrow it will be one country or another. The Zionist plan is limitless. After Palestine, the Zionists aspire to expand from the Nile to the Euphrates. When they will have digested the region they overtook, they will aspire to further expansion, and so on. Their plan is embodied in the 'Protocols of the Elders of Zion,' and their present conduct is the best proof of what we are saying."; accessed May 2017.

133. Islamic Antisemitism in Historical Perspective (PDF), Anti-Defamation League, 276 kB; accessed October 2013.

134. Omri Ceren, "O Beloved Belgium, Sacred Land of Anti-Semitism," *Commentary Magazine*, May 17, 2011, http://www.commentarymagazine.com/2011/05/17/belgian-minister-says-to-forget-about-nazis/; accessed July 2017.

135. Oren Dorell, "Tiny Belgium is a terrorist crossroad," *USA Today*, January 17, 2015, http://www.usatoday.com/story/news/world/2015/01/16/belgium-terrorist-crossroad/21866187/; accessed December 2016.

136. John Goldingay, *Isaiah* (Grand Rapids, MI, Baker Books, 2001), 223.

137. Walter Brueggemann, *Isaiah 40–66* (Louisville, KY: Westminster John Knox Press, 1998), 18.

138. Barry Rubin, "The Region: All Israel, All the Time," *The Jerusalem Post*, August 23, 2010, http://www.jpost.com/Opinion/Op-Ed-Contributors/The-Region-All-Israel-all-the-time; accessed October 2016.

139. http://wcc-coe.org/wcc/news/press/01/43pu.html; accessed July 2017.

140. Ibid

141. Quoted by George Gilder in *The Israel Test* (Minneapolis, MN: Richard Vigilante Books, 2009), 22.

142. Arthur W. Pink (1886–1952), "The Death of the Firstborn, pt. 1," Old Testament Study: Exodus 11:1–10, http://www.scripturestudies.com/Vol11/K10/ot.html; accessed November 2016.

BOOKS BY: MIKE EVANS

Israel: America's Key to Survival

Save Jerusalem

The Return

Jerusalem D.C.

Purity and Peace of Mind

Who Cries for the Hurting?

Living Fear Free

I Shall Not Want

Let My People Go

Jerusalem Betrayed

Seven Years of Shaking: A Vision

The Nuclear Bomb of Islam

Jerusalem Prophecies

Pray For Peace of Jerusalem

America's War:
   The Beginning of the End

The Jerusalem Scroll

The Prayer of David

The Unanswered Prayers of Jesus

God Wrestling

The American Prophecies 20ᵗ

Beyond Iraq: The Next Move

The Final Move beyond Iraq

Showdown with Nuclear Iran 2006

Jimmy Carter: The Liberal Left
   and World Chaos

Atomic Iran

Cursed

Betrayed

The Light— his life

Corrie's Reflections & Meditations

The Revolution

The Final Generation

Seven Days

The Locket

Persia: The Final Jihad

GAMECHANGER SERIES:

GameChanger

Samson Option

The Four Horsemen

THE PROTOCOLS SERIES:

The Protocols

The Candidate

Jerusalem

The History of Christian Zionism

Countdown

Ten Boom: Betsie, Promise of God

Commanded Blessing

Born Again: 1948

Born Again: 1967

Presidents in Prophecy

Stand with Israel

Prayer, Power and Purpose

Turning Your Pain Into Gain

Christopher Columbus, Secret Jew

Living in the F.O.G.

Finding Favor with God

Finding Favor with Man

Unleashing God's Favor

The Jewish State: The Volunteers

See You in New York

Friends of Zion:
  Patterson & Wingate

The Columbus Code

The Temple

Satan, You Can't Have
  My Country!

Satan, You Can't Have Israel!

Lights in the Darkness

The Seven Feasts of Israel

Netanyahu

Jew-Hatred and the Church

The Visionaries

Why Was I Born?

Son, I Love You

√ Jerusalem DC (David's Capital)

√ Israel Reborn read 2019

√ Prayer, a conversation c God 2018

COMING SOON:

√ Shimon Peres: A Friend of Zion

The New-Hitler 2019

The good Father 2019

TO PURCHASE, CONTACT: orders@timeworthybooks.com
P. O. BOX 30000, PHOENIX, AZ 85046

MICHAEL DAVID EVANS, the #1 *New York Times* bestselling author, is an award-winning journalist/Middle East analyst. Dr. Evans has appeared on hundreds of network television and radio shows including *Good Morning America, Crossfire* and *Nightline,* and *The Rush Limbaugh Show,* and on Fox Network, *CNN World News,* NBC, ABC, and CBS. His articles have been published in the *Wall Street Journal, USA Today, Washington Times, Jerusalem Post* and newspapers worldwide. More than twenty-five million copies of his books are in print, and he is the award-winning producer of nine documentaries based on his books.

Dr. Evans is considered one of the world's leading experts on Israel and the Middle East, and is one of the most sought-after speakers on that subject. He is the chairman of the board of the ten Boom Holocaust Museum in Haarlem, Holland, and is the founder of Israel's first Christian museum located in the Friends of Zion Heritage Center in Jerusalem.

Dr. Evans has authored a number of books including: *History of Christian Zionism, Showdown with Nuclear Iran, Atomic Iran, The Next Move Beyond Iraq, The Final Move Beyond Iraq,* and *Countdown.* His body of work also includes the novels *Seven Days, GameChanger, The Samson Option, The Four Horsemen, The Locket, Born Again: 1967,* and *The Columbus Code.*

✦ ✦ ✦

Michael David Evans is available to speak or for interviews.
Contact: EVENTS@drmichaeldevans.com.